*The American
Immigration Collection*

The Mexican
in
the United States

EMORY S. BOGARDUS

Arno Press and The New York Times

NEW YORK 1970

Reprint Edition 1970 by Arno Press Inc.

Reprinted from a copy in
The University of Illinois Library

LC# 70-129389
ISBN 0-405-00575-X

The American Immigration Collection—Series II
ISBN for complete set 0-405-00543-1

Manufactured in the United States of America

UNIVERSITY

OF

SOUTHERN CALIFORNIA

SCHOOL OF RESEARCH STUDIES NUMBER FIVE

SOCIAL SCIENCE SERIES   NUMBER EIGHT

THE MEXICAN IN THE UNITED STATES

By

EMORY S. BOGARDUS, PH.D.

Professor of Sociology
University of Southern California

UNIVERSITY OF SOUTHERN CALIFORNIA PRESS

LOS ANGELES, 1934

PREFACE

Of all human relations, the field of race relations is outstandingly interesting. Its study throws new light on the comprehension of social conflicts and adjustments generally. Moreover, a consideration of Mexican immigrants and of their problems in the United States illuminates the nature of many phases of race relations.

Now is a favorable time to discuss the problems of Mexican immigrants dispassionately. Mexican immigration to the United States has run a cycle. A number of chapters in this population movement are concluded for the time being, and hence they may be considered as completed units. During the period of the depression when economic interest in Mexicans is low, social interest may assume a more rational viewpoint than usual and engage in plans not only for solving current problems relative to Mexican immigrants but for anticipating another tide of Mexican immigration when economic prosperity returns. It is quite certain that with a new period of economic development in the United States thousands of Mexicans will seek admittance. Hence it will be wise to consider the Mexican immigrant's problems before they grow serious again.

This particular study is based on new and first-hand materials, such as life histories, interview data, psycho-social analyses. The actual experiences of Mexican immigrants together with the definition and interpretation of these experiences that are made by Mexicans are drawn upon heavily. The configuration of the personality of the Mexican is given consideration in terms of his experiences and his interpretations of said experiences. The point of view is organismic rather than atomistic; it is configurational rather than segmentary.

One of the best ways to understand the Mexican immigrant is to enter into the social situations which he has known in Mexico and in the United States. In this way one can learn to feel as the Mexican feels and to comprehend the meaning of his problems when he migrates from his country into ours. A number of short excerpts from life history documents of

Mexican immigrants will be introduced for illustrative purposes and will afford the reader an open sesame to some of the fascinating, colorful, and picturesque problems of racial conflict and adjustment.

Special thanks are due the many persons, research workers, home teachers, public officials, agriculturists and other employers, and Mexican immigrants, in short, all who have made this study possible. The work was extended over a number of years and has involved many difficulties, but it will have been worth while if it results in a better understanding of the Mexican immigrants by citizens of the United States.

University of Southern California   EMORY S. BOGARDUS
Los Angeles, California
March 1, 1934

TABLE OF CONTENTS

CHAPTER I

TYPES AND BACKGROUNDS

THE MEXICAN in the United States ranges from a broadly cultured person to a low-grade illiterate. It is the latter who unfortunately furnishes the stereotype that most "Americans"[1] think of when the word Mexican is mentioned. But there are many types of Mexicans in the United States, each possessing distinctive backgrounds and interesting characteristics. Like any other racial group, violence is done them if they are lumped together. They need to be viewed according to any other group —in personal terms. In consequence they are found to run the gamut from low- to high-grade persons and are to be judged accordingly.

Naturally, the native-born Mexican of several generations' standing may be presented first. He antedates the United States. In other words, Mexicans were natives in the Southwest for decades when the region was still a part of Mexico. Hence, it is not surprising that today some of the descendants of these old-time Mexicans feel a certain aristocracy of spirit which they are unable to express. It is natural, therefore, that there should be some native-born Mexicans in the Southwest who cannot help thinking of citizens of the United States as the real immigrants and as persons who have thrust themselves and their aggressive civilization upon a siesta-loving people. Many of these historic Mexicans are largely of Indian origin; some still live in primitive fashion. They are citizens of the United States by birth, but Mexican and Indian by culture. They are often erroneously confused with recent immigrants. In Texas, for example, they are sometimes known as "Texanos" or descendants of the original Texas Mexicans.[2] While not all

---

[1] Unfortunately, there is no single term that refers to the citizens of the United States. The term, American, is so used, to be sure, but improperly, for it also includes everyone resident in either North or South America. Hence the term "American" will be put in quotation marks to designate the people of the United States.

[2] L. C. Harby, "Texan Types and Contrasts," *Harpers Magazine*, 81: 229-46.

play a backward rôle, their total influence in the United States is not great. Sometimes they form population nuclei to which recent Mexican immigrants migrate, although they do not like as a class to be mistaken for the newcomers; they feel that they are "above" the latter.

On the whole, these Spanish-Americans, as they are often called, are misunderstood by other citizens of the United States. They are not distinguished by some "Americans" from recent Mexican immigrants. They are descendants in the main of persons who long ago migrated across the Rio Grande and located in territory occupied by more or less hostile Indians. As in the case of many other immigrants, they left their antecedent homes in order to escape oppression. They elected to struggle with the Indians rather than accept peonage in Old Mexico. They have forged ahead and some of their representatives have reached the state legislature in New Mexico. They carry on conversation and on occasion make public speeches in Spanish.

A three-cornered culture situation often obtains. The new Mexican immigrants do not always identify themselves with the Spanish-Americans. The latter are farmers who own their own lands and who view the newcomers kindly because of similarity of language and traditions but who do not want to be confused with the incoming peons. The Anglo-Americans, the Spanish-Americans, and the Mexican immigrants comprise an interesting ecological combination, but are not as yet a successful integration of peoples.

The real problem is the conflict between Spanish-Americans and Anglo-Americans. This arises from religious differences (Catholicism versus Protestantism), and from political reasons. It is reported that in some sections only Spanish-Americans can be elected to office and in others, only Anglo-Americans. It is unfortunate that Spanish-Americans although "American-born" for three or four generations are still not well assimilated.

The Spanish-Americans are loyal as a class to the United States. The public schools are doing important acculturation work. Many of the younger Spanish-Americans will soon be ready to drop the "Spanish" from their classification. Even these, however, are often made to feel the evil effects of Nordic arrogance. Indifference sometimes characterizes the relations between Anglo-Americans and Spanish-Americans. Clearly, a lack of common interest is uppermost. It is not strange that a great deal of "smoldering resentment" still obtains. The attitudes of certain Spanish-Americans have been interestingly likened to those of the Scotch and English mountaineers of eastern Kentucky and Tennessee. Little real coöperation and a great deal of political and religious competition occur.

A second group of people in the United States that needs to be distinguished from recent Mexican immigrants is composed of those who belong to aristocratic Spanish families. They are descendants of families who were leaders in the Southwest in early days. They came when the Southwest belonged to Mexico. They were the social, political, and economic élite. After them some of the cities and many of the important streets of the cities of the Southwest were named. Today, some represent the fading glory of a ruling past. Some cling to the old-time status in an entirely new age.[3]

Partially related are the Spanish-Mexicans of recent migration. This third group is composed of persons who have fled from revolutions in Mexico to special sections not only in the Southwest but in many of the large cities of the United States. Most of them are political refugees. Recent political tendencies in Mexico have deprived them of status, and they lead a restless life in the United States. Unlike the descendants of the original Spanish and Mexicans in the United States who expect to stay here, these Spanish-Mexican refugees look forward to returning to Mexico to live, although many doubtless will never do so. They have few contacts with Mexican immigrant peons.[4]

More important than any of the three Mexican types so far mentioned are the educated Mexicans who are representatives of the current ruling people of Mexico. Many are young men who are alert and progressive. They are the products of acculturation processes in Mexico and in the United States. They

[3] For an excellent statement concerning the early Spanish and Mexican history of the Southwest, see *A Short History of California*, by R. D. Hunt and Nellie Van de Grift Sanchez (New York: Thomas Y. Crowell Company, 1929), particularly Parts II and III.

[4] Max S. Handman, "The Mexican Immigrant in Texas," *Southwestern Political and Social Science Quarterly*, 7:33 ff; also G. Bromley Oxnam, "Mexicans in Los Angeles from the Standpoint of the Religious Forces of the City," *Annals of the American Academy of Political and Social Science*, 93:130-33.

do not rely on Spanish ancestry for status; in fact some are ashamed of their Spanish lineage. They resent being called Spanish and wish to be known as Mexican. They explain that there is a new Mexican civilization in their home country, similar to the new American civilization developing out of race mixtures in the United States. A new Mexican culture is the nucleus of the thinking of this type of Mexican immigrant. They are in the United States temporarily, for purposes of study and travel. Their loyalty is to Mexico; they parallel, somewhat, Americans who are living temporarily in foreign countries for a variety of special reasons.

These Mexicans are interested in the welfare of unskilled Mexicans in the United States. They feel a responsibility for the welfare of their less fortunate compatriots. They are important because of the rôle they may play in effecting interracial adjustments. They may serve in a liaison capacity between unskilled Mexican laborers and "American" employers in industry and agriculture. As a rule, they are liberal in thought, impatient with injustice, sympathetic with labor rather than with capital, and favor dynamic social change rather than social stagnation.

The Mexican consuls, attachés, and their families constitute an important section of this group. As political appointees they lead circumspect lives. They specialize on extending political courtesies. They are usually well-liked by American leaders whom they contact. They are in close touch with unskilled and other Mexican immigrants who get into trouble in the United States. In this capacity they come to know a great deal about the hardships suffered by Mexican laborers in our country. They secure redress for wrongs inflicted on Mexican laborers; they help individual Mexicans out of predicaments, but are naturally loath to take a part in economic or social life in the United States.

There remains to be discussed the largest of all the groups of Mexican immigrants, the unskilled laborers who have immigrated in recent years. This fifth group is the most significant industrially, socially, politically. In the succeeding chapters of this study the unskilled Mexican will be discussed, unless references are specifically made to one of the other four groups.

The typical Mexican unskilled laborer has come into the United States annually in considerable numbers, for the past twenty years or more, and particularly since the World War closed. When the immigration of unskilled laborers from Europe was definitely limited in 1921, employers in the United States, especially in the Southwest, turned their eyes toward Mexico. In fact, it has been asserted that Mexicans were not included in the quota list of countries in 1921, or in 1924, at the special urge of employers of "cheap labor." Moreover, it is clear that employers have sought labor from south of the Border.

An examination of Table I reveals the fact that Mexican immigration is no new phenomenon.[5] In the early decades of the last century when southwestern United States was a part of Mexico there was a considerable influx to Texas and contiguous portions of the United States. The Civil War period naturally is reflected in a decrease. A subsequent rise was followed by the unparalleled low figures for the closing decade of the nineteenth century.

TABLE I

MEXICAN IMMIGRATION TO THE UNITED STATES

Year	Number	Per Cent of Total Immigration
1820-30	4,818	3.2
1831-40	6,599	1.1
1841-50	3,271	.2
1851-60	3,078	.1
1861-70	2,191	.1
1871-80	5,162	.2
1881-90	1,913	-
1891-01	971	-
1901-10	49,642	.6
1911-20	219,004	3.8
1921-30	459,259	11.1

Table II gives the figures, year by year, beginning with 1911.[6] The figures are relatively significant and stable until the postwar years, when they take a leap. They change little during the World War period. The decreases in 1921 and 1922 are followed by another jump, reaching a climax in 1924. In the

---

[5] Annual Report, Commissioner General of Immigration, Washington, D.C., 1928, p. 190.

[6] From Annual Reports of the Commissioner General of Immigration, Washington, D. C.

gives the figures of Mexican emigration from the United States.[11]

The United States Census for 1930 gives the Mexican population of the United States as 1,422,533, or over one twelfth of the total Mexican population of the world. According to the census instructions in 1930 "all persons born in Mexico or having parents born in Mexico, who are definitely not white, Negro, Indian, Chinese, or Japanese, should be returned as Mexican." If the census figures for 1920 had been computed on the 1930 basis, there would have been 700,541 individuals classified as Mexican at that time. Even so, the increase in Mexicans for the decade was 721,992, or more than 100 per cent. The ratio in 1930 of male to female for the whole country for Mexicans was 114.3. If the United States be divided roughly into North, South, and West, then the ratio of Mexican males to females was 165.6, 106.1, and 116.9, respectively. The ten states with the largest Mexican population in 1930 are given in Table IV.

TABLE IV

MEXICANS IN THE UNITED STATES BY STATES, 1930 (U. S. CENSUS)

	State	Number		State	Number
1.	Texas	683,681	6.	Illinois	28,906
2.	California	368,013	7.	Michigan	13,336
3.	Arizona	114,173	8.	Indiana	9,642
4.	New Mexico	59,340	9.	Oklahoma	7,354
5.	Colorado	57,676	10.	Wyoming	7,174

Racially, the great bulk of Mexican immigrants belong to the mestizo class. In the mestizo, or the mixture of Indian and Spaniard, the Indian elements are dominant. The mestizo child was raised largely by his Indian mother and hence reflects his Indian cultural backgrounds to a large degree.

Economically, the Mexican immigrant has represented chiefly the peon or serf on the hacienda. He has lived in the plantation or hacienda village and has been fashioned into a more or less docile and dependent creature rather than into a free, independent person. As a class he has not come from the larger Mexican city or from the many Indian villages, but from

11 From Annual Reports of the Commissioner of Immigration.

the benevolent paternalism of the hacienda where he did not learn that his soul was his own and where he could not escape a servile relationship.

Religiously, he is partly a product of Roman Catholic influence, and partly a product of the nature-worshiping religions of his Indian ancestors. He has believed in the supernatural. He is a believer in a mystical rather than in a scientific interpretation of religion. Symbolism plays a large rôle in his life.

Domestically, his life centers in the family and many children. He is the patriarchal head of his household. A common picture in the villages is that of a man, his wife holding a small child in her arms, other children running about, and the omnipresent beast of burden, a burro.

Politically, his loyalty is extended concretely to the local community, and symbolically, to Mexico as a whole. His loyalty to his native soil is deep-seated. He has known so much oppression that he either accepts the status quo without question or else he breaks forth in revolutionary activities.

Personally, he does not find his highest expression in acquiring things or in getting material wealth. In the words of Mary Austin,[12] he finds the highest expression of his personality in music and songs and dances, in pottery-making and manners, in the enjoyment of the only certain possession that we have, namely, the present, and in making and creating, not in owning.

---

12 Mary Austin, "Mexicans and New Mexico," *Survey,* 66:144.

CHAPTER II

COMMUNITY AND CAMP LIFE

Further light is cast on the major group of Mexicans in the United States, particularly on those of the unskilled labor groups, by considering their community life. Differences in culture patterns distinguish certain Mexican immigrant communities from each other as well as from other communities in the United States.

In the first place there is the metropolitan type of Mexican community, such as the one located in the center of old Los Angeles. This was known as the Plaza district, which was already in existence long before the United States was established, and which flourished until recently. Nearly one half of the history of this metropolitan concentration of Mexicans has been a part of the history of Spain and Mexico. Its people for several decades were citizens of Spain and Mexico and regarded the people of the United States as foreigners. Despite a church more than a century old, a plaza, and other historic institutions, the district is now undergoing serious disorganization. Modern industry "invaded" the region, land values climbed upward, housing and living conditions went downward, and Mexicans began to move out. More recently Los Angeles has undertaken to extend its Civic Center District into the Plaza area. San Antonio, El Paso, and other cities have central Mexican areas undergoing somewhat similar changes.[1]

In these metropolitan areas personal disorganization is great; social problems abound. The Mexican and his family are insuperably handicapped in the same way that all persons and families who live in the disorganizing zones of transition in large cities are defeated. To understand the social situations of Mexicans so located, it is necessary to know the sociology of the city.

---

[1] These areas have become a part of "zones of transition" as described by Park and Burgess, *The City* (Chicago: University of Chicago Press, 1925), Chapter II.

A second type of Mexican community bears a complementary relation to the first. It is an area of second or third settlement, sometimes located within the zone of transition and sometimes in a suburban district. Even in a city of thirty thousand population there are often two or three areas of second settlement, and an area or two of third settlement. In S—, interestingly enough, one of the areas of second settlement was started by young married Mexican couples, who had outgrown the original Mexican area "beyond the tracks," and who sought better living conditions and higher status. From this area, another or third has developed sporadically.

Sometimes the Mexican areas of second settlement are developed by real estate promoters. Mexicans are induced to leave the disreputable housing conditions of the area of first settlement and to move several miles into a suburban area of open country, passing by other areas of second settlement. This phenomenon is apparently induced by opportunities to buy a few square yards of ground and to own a home, no matter how humble.

A third type of community is represented by groups of Mexicans living in small cities or towns. Sometimes fifty, a hundred, or more families are found living in a segregated section of a city or small town. They are characterized by a simple community life and by a lack of adequate social organization. A considerable percentage of the Mexicans in the United States live under some such conditions.

In G—, there is a Mexican population of several thousand, located in a section extending through the center of the city and dividing it into two parts. The Mexican community is the original settlement, dates back for more than a century, and contains a historic mission. Anglo-Americans and others have settled both to the north and the south. The old business center of the city, located in the central Mexican community, is being supplemented by two or three other business centers in the English-speaking sections of the city. According to a survey made in the prosperity year of 1928 when approximately every fifth Mexican family was called on, about two fifths of the families owned or were paying on their homes. About one third of the men had steady employment while two thirds depended on chance employment, seasonal labor, and hence had been out of employment practically all of the pre-ceding winter.[2] While living conditions were classed on the whole as good, several bad spots were found, characterized by overcrowding and poor housing. The worst housing conditions existed where citizens of the United States rented to Mexicans. "In all cases where the people [Mexicans] were buying or owned their homes, the houses and yards were in much better condition than where the people were renting." When the question was asked of a family if the members expected to move soon, the answer was generally, "No." The stationary character of the population was noticeable; this community is one of the oldest centers in the Southwest for Spanish-speaking peoples. "The oldest family connection was found to be an old Mexican couple who have lived here 88 years . . . . . There is a number of early Spanish-speaking families who have histories dating back several generations here." [3]

In D—, there is a number of Mexican families living out-side the main Mexican settlement in a dozen different spots, usually as single families or perhaps in groups of two families. It would require an ecological study in order to predict which of these Mexican families are likely to become the nucleus of a new Mexican area.

In another small city, the Mexicans live in the center of town. They came long ago; they were first. "Americans" moved from a nearby city and built fine homes and estab-lished a business district. They are now striving to remove the Mexicans, as the Mexican area is judged to be an "eyesore." Some want "to drive the Mexicans out." A part of the Mexican area is owned by "Americans" who are holding their lots for higher prices and who prefer to rent to Mexicans. The Mexicans themselves are not particularly disturbed by their situation.

In E—, where seven different sections were canvassed in 1928 and a total of 982 adults and of 1,428 children were studied, it was found that 887 of the adults, or 90 per cent, were born in Mexico, while 1,074 of the children, or 75.2 per cent, were born in the United States, thus indicating a large second-generation group, which is experiencing according to preliminary

---

2 Survey conducted by P. G. W.

3 From interview materials submitted by P. G. W.

studies a number of serious adjustment problems in the country of their birth. Of 482 families considered, it was found that only 47 had resided in the United States less than five years, that only 90 had lived here from five to ten years, and that 345 families, or 71.2 per cent, had been residents ten years and over. The relative permanence involved is especially important when it is considered that less than five per cent of the adults (foreign-born) are naturalized or had taken steps to that end. Of the 470 houses surveyed, about one-half (230) were owned by the Mexican occupants. Over one-half (271) were "well-kept." Of the 482 families, 220 or nearly one half were classified as employed, 103 were working on ranches and farms as laborers, 99 at general labor, 20 as sales people, and 29 were found to be owning and operating business establishments. Twenty families were described as "having no permanent home" but as "following the crops."[4]

Sometimes a Mexican community is located just outside the city limits. Conditions are usually very poor, for there is little social control. Both personal and social disorganization ranks high; in fact, so high that sometimes the areas are nuisances. The nearby city residents, however, are helpless. In one instance a movement has been inaugurated to buy certain city blocks and move the Mexicans into the area, so that better control might be exercised. In this way it is proposed to do away with the disreputable area outside the city limits.

The fourth type of Mexican community is represented by "camps." These fall into several types. One is in reality a small and isolated Mexican neighborhood; it is hardly large enough to be called a community; it scarcely seems complete or permanent enough to be called a neighborhood. It might be labeled a permanent temporary quarters. Disorganization is common.

Another type of Mexican camp is found in connection with railroad work. Every railroad town has its section house; and every section house, its Mexican families. The Mexican dooryards usually have at least a few bright flowers, even though the tracks are near by and one or more engines are puffing away while passengers or freight are being unloaded. Conveniences are few and life is routine. Congestion is not uncommon.

Then one day my husband got a job with the L. Railroad and we were to move to A—. It was no trouble to move, for we had practically nothing to bring. When we landed in A—, we were sent to the railroad company

---

4 From materials submitted by N. E. B. and A. K.

house. It had one room and a very small kitchen. The ten of us lived there for eight months, in one room. In Mexico we had had four rooms. It was a dirty house, and although the Company was to furnish the house there was not a single mattress, only sacks on the beds. All of us could not lie down at once. We slept in turns. We had never done this in Mexico.[5]

Then, there are "model camps" which are found on large ranches owned by men who have become business-farmers and who have learned that it "pays" to do "welfare work" for their Mexican laborers. Often such a camp is built like a barracks, with accommodations for a large number of families. Control is exercised over sanitation, and a home teacher is employed, sometimes by the public school and sometimes by the company. One of her first duties is to discover dissatisfaction and to keep the Mexicans contented. The following excerpt refers to a Mexican woman who functions as a "peacemaker" in a Mexican camp for an "American" landlord.

Mrs. E. has for a number of years lived in the same small house in a group of Mexican hovels. She is well loved by all her friends. She is generous and always has time for anyone who is in need or in sorrow. She has unlimited curiosity and nothing goes on in the neighborhood that she does not know. She has a ring-side seat in all the quarrels and happenings, festivities or group gatherings of her neighborhood. She is the "vital statistics" column, the "You and Your Friend" column of an unpublished newspaper for this Mexican group. Her neighbors go to her not so much for advice as for news. She is an authority on births, deaths, marriages, and the encounters of her friends with priests, preachers, or officers of the law.

The group of houses which constitutes her neighborhood are owned by a certain American who rents them at a low fee. Because Mrs. E. knows so many Mexicans, because she is so interested in everyone and everything, because she is well liked, this Anglo-American landlord for six years has given her her rent free, in order that she may keep peace in the neighborhood and keep all the tenants as contented as possible. She thinks she is earning her rent, and perhaps she is, for once a week she collects the rent from all the tenants and takes it to her landlord. To insure safety for this money she conceals it in an old stocking which she pins securely in her bosom, underneath her dress.[6]

The community organization of each of these four major types of Mexican communities is exceedingly simple, whether

---

[5] From interview materials submitted by G. A. S.
[6] From interview materials submitted by H. W. W.

viewed administratively or sociologically.[7] Community organization in the administrative sense is largely missing, for the Mexican peon has had little opportunity to learn about or to participate in anything of the kind.

That Mexicans can develop along this line is evident from their response to coöperative programs, including the Blue Cross.[8] In B—, for example, the Mexicans several years ago organized to care for the needy among their own number, and succeeded well. Mexicans have a responsive, communal nature which gives a good basis for the programs of community agencies.

In a more sociological sense, community organization relates to the underlying type of social life. In this sense, the community or social organization of Mexican immigrant life is pristine. The family, aside from the church, is the chief center of control. The Mexican's basic community organization of life is not of the efficient Japanese type; neither is it of the industrial-individualistic American form. On the other hand, it differs widely from the family clan-village Chinese form of community organization. It is an unorganized, loose arrangement, resting on daily needs, and taking little thought of the morrow.

In consequence, the Mexican immigrant is easily subject to manipulation by that type of person who exploits uneducated workers. The Mexican peon has fallen victim to the wiles of liquor sellers and of dope sellers, and to promoters of wild-cat schemes of one kind and another; his wages have often been extracted from him by the clever devices of the unscrupulous. Sometimes the less scrupulous among his fellow countrymen have taken advantage of him. However, he has fine possibilities of developing an active and helpful community life, especially when educated and trained to that end. In fact his possibilities in this direction, because of his communal backgrounds, are as good if not better than those of individualistic "Americans" of the same culture levels.

---

[7] For a discussion of this distinction, see J. F. Steiner, *Community Organization* (New York: The Century Company, 1925), Ch. XX.

[8] A counterpart of the Red Cross.

CHAPTER III

FAMILY LIFE AND CONDITIONS

The family life and conditions of the mass of Mexican immigrants are largely representative of the culture traits of the lower culture classes in any country. It is necessary first of all to consider the Mexican immigrant in the light of the family culture traits of the peon classes in Mexico. The marriage ceremony, for instance, has not always been observed among the poorer classes, because it has been priced too high. Not being able to afford it, the Mexican peon has got along without it. It has been a luxury. It has been considered desirable, but not essential, because of its expensiveness.

Therefore, the Mexican immigrant laborer is not necessarily to be judged immoral, if he has neglected the marriage ceremony in living with his chosen and accepted wife. Many people in the United States are naturally shocked when they learn that certain Mexicans live together as husband and wife, without having been officially married, and without feeling any particular sense of shame or guilt. In view of the culture traits, this procedure is doubtless natural. After having lived together for a number of years Mexicans sometimes marry, when they are urged to do so by a priest or other friend. When they learn of their "duty," they usually respond, but many consider the ceremony as a form of secondary significance.

The father views large numbers of children carelessly. Again, the attitude is quite primitive. If the children become too numerous and the burden of feeding these hungry mouths too heavy, the father may desert. The mother, like all true mothers, stands faithfully by, shouldering the burdens alone, the best that she may. Parental irresponsibility on the part of the father and "maternal instinct" on the part of the mother sum up the family situation for the lowest levels of Mexican immigrants.

The mother may take a somewhat fatalistic attitude. If she be religiously trained, she is likely to view her brood as gifts from God. Her fatalism is illustrated by her belief that one child more or one less does not matter. If a baby dies, it is God's will; there is one less mouth to feed; there will be "another one along soon." A high infant mortality rate is not viewed by the mother with alarm. Loyalty to home, maternal feelings, frequent washing of clothes—these reactions stand out.

If 1928 may be taken as a somewhat typical year, then, by California counties, the following birth rate figures are significant. Imperial, 52.0 per thousand Mexicans; San Bernardino, 44.5; Riverside, 43.6; Ventura, 39.5; Orange, 38.3; Madera, 33.9; Santa Barbara, 33.8; San Diego, 31.5; Los Angeles, 26.3; others, lower. The variations are to be accounted for by a number of factors, such as distance from the Border and the percentage of women to the total Mexican population, social and health work being done for the Mexicans, and urbanization. In nearly every case the Mexican birth rate is lower for the county seat or large city than for the counties in which these cities are located. For example, the birth rate for the County of Los Angeles was "26.3 per thousand Mexicans, and for the City, 22.7; for the County of San Bernardino, 44.5, and for the City, 34.2; for the County of San Diego, 31.5, and for the City, 17.5." [1]

The infant mortality rate for Mexicans for the same year was almost fifteen per cent compared with a little over six per cent for other races. There were 2,050 deaths of Mexican infants out of a total of 13,846 Mexican births. This high mortality rate, according to Dr. W. H. Dickie, is due to: (1) ignorance; (2) lack of cleanliness; (3) lack of care; (4) lack of proper feeding.[2]

For Mexican peons there has been little if any training in sex matters. Sex relations are primitive. The response, however, to education and training is noticeable among the second generation, and also among Mexican immigrant women. The birth control movement makes slow progress because of religious opposition.

---

[1] From the Report of Dr. W. M. Dickie, Director of the Department of Public Health, State of California, to the Governor, for 1928.

[2] Loc. cit.

The birth rate is high, in fact higher than a family of four or five children would indicate, because of the high infant mortality rate. Some mothers, however, are beginning to protest against large families and to inquire how they may protect themselves. Some of those who attend classes in English are particularly in earnest in this matter. Occasionally a Mexican man in the peon class is awakening to the evils of an unregulated birth rate. A growing trend is indicated by the Mexican woman who advised her Americanization teacher not to be in a hurry in getting married on the ground of "much work, too much children." A Mexican father admits: "I getta married too young. My wife too young. I am glad that she [his daughter] wait awhile. It is too hard when you are too young." Another Mexican makes the explanation: "No, we have no children. Too much work. One baby, then another baby. Too many. They get sick. Too bad. We don't want too many children."

When they came to the United States they had just one *muchacha*, but now, six, Mrs. R. informs me, calling in her brood for the visitor's inspection. Sophia, Maria, etc., and she names them all to me, as I smile at them. Her husband wants a boy. "I got enough children." And I could see by her tired face that she had enough to do, with a family of its present size.

"Have you *esposa?*" she asked me, being curious about my family. "Oh no! Don't get *esposa,* too *mucho trabajo. Mucho muchachos."* (Don't get husband, much work, too many children.)[3]

Despite the burden of bearing many children and the lack of advantages, the urge for a better way of living is still active. The teachers of Mexican mothers report many instances of deep-seated longing.

"Do you like to live here?" I asked her. "Yes, *muy bien!* Business very bad now, though," was her answer. "All Mexicans go away pick grapes. No work here. No business for my husband. Taxes *mucho dinero.* Business bad! Taxes *mucho.* Very hard."

"Are your children in school?" I asked. *"Dos,"* she answered. "Like it *mucho.* I like *mucho,* too. I like you come." And her kind, genuine hospitality and eagerness to concentrate in spite of other things—on our lesson in English each afternoon, was real testimony of her interest in her work.

She, a woman of 29 years, as a girl employed in a laundry with no home environment, married to a pool room proprietor, mother of six children, no

---

[3] From interview materials submitted by G. A. S.

educational advantages, poverty stricken, a stranger in a strange land. But still smiling, eager, longing for a chance to learn, and be somebody. What could be more challenging?[4]

In the picture of a better class peon home that is given in the following excerpt, the Mexican's love of color and the simplicity of appointments are the two most noticeable factors.

Mrs. E. and her husband are lovers of flowers, and their small front yard is a gay and colorful mixture of many varieties. Their two room house is more or less neatly kept. The usual "treasure corner" is in evidence in the front room. In this "treasure corner" are flowers made of paper, candles, pictures of Mother Mary and the Babe, picture postcards, bright colored bits of paper, a colored picture or two from magazine advertisements, in fact everything is placed with care and reverence in the "treasure corner." Above her front door in this room are an American flag and a Mexican flag. A bed, a table, an old victrola comprise the furniture of the front room. A stove, a chair, a table, cupboard, and several boxes furnish the back room. No matter how poor her furnishings, Mrs. E. is always hospitable.[5]

Another word picture may be included of what a poor but higher level Mexican peon home is like. The following description is indicative of the developments that occur when adequate opportunities are afforded.

The D. home is unpretentious. They have four rooms. The furnishings are better than in most Mexican peon homes. The front room is furnished as I said with a piano, several very comfortable, though inexpensive chairs, one of which is a rocker, and a bright colored rug covers the floor. It is cheap and gaudy but it is a rug. Neat, clean curtains hang at the windows. There are beds and dressers in both bedrooms, small rugs on both floors. The kitchen has its oil stove, table, and cupboard. Everything is immaculately clean, even the yard is swept until it is smooth and hard. Flowerbeds of many colorful varieties are planted between the house and the nearest neighbor's place.[6]

Mexicans try to improve their living conditions by moving from one neighborhood to a better one. However, when they leave the Mexican neighborhood for a higher-class American one, they are usually doomed to disappointment. They have to contend with the prejudices of "Americans." A Mexican makes the following report about certain friends of hers.

---

[4] Loc. cit.

[5] Loc. cit.

[6] From interview materials submitted by H. W. W.

They bought a new stucco house, but there is a very bad American who lives next door. The American says bad things to her, and calls her a "dirty Mexican," and she is just as clean as clean can be. My friend only live three months there. She was so happy with her new house, she fixed it up so cute, and it was a nice house. They planted garden, flowers, and lawn. She worked all day to make it nice, but the American make her sick, she is not happy there, she wants to move now.[7]

The Mexican mother shows her strong maternal impulses in attempting to safeguard her daughters when they reach adolescent and marriageable ages. Conflicting culture traits cause havoc. In Mexico, girls are chaperoned. No girl or young woman would go out alone in the evening, or to a party without the chaperonage of an older person. In the United States the opposite rule prevails. American girls go unchaperoned to parties with young men; Mexican girls respond with a bound to such freedom. They swing quickly from one extreme to the other, with the result that the mother often fails when she tries to maintain Mexican standards. The more closely she safeguards the daughters, the stronger becomes the desire of the girls to enjoy American freedom, without realizing their lack of training for such freedom or the consequent dangers. "This terrible freedom in America" is the bane of the Mexican mother's life.

There is one thing which still seems strange to Mrs. E. She says she will never get used to it, and that is the freedom which our women enjoy. She still cannot understand how women can go unaccompanied on the street, or how they can go about to and from their homes and their work alone.

"It is because they can run around so much and be so free, that our Mexican girls do not know how to act. So many girls run away and get married. This terrible freedom in this United States. The Mexican girls seeing American girls with freedom, they want it too, so they go where they like. They do not mind their parents; this terrible freedom. But what can the Mexican mothers do? It is the custom, and we cannot change it, but it is bad. I do not have to worry because I have no daughters, but the poor *senoras* with many girls, they worry. I only had three sons; they are gone now, they have been dead many years."[8]

An observant Mexican immigrant mother feels that the Mexican family is superior to the American. While she recog-

---

7 *Loc. cit.*
8 From interview materials submitted by G. A. S.

nizes the weaknesses of Mexican homes, yet they do not seem to her to be as serious as the disintegration that appears to be taking place in American families.

The thing that shocked me most about the United States was the lack of solidarity in the home. The American children do not have much regard for their parents. I was renting in an American home where there were four daughters from nine to sixteen years of age and every one of them was out until three o'clock at night. Their parents had no control over them. In Mexico I had to be in at eight o'clock with my father and mother. But here it is different. Of course it makes for individuality and independence. They learn to think for themselves, but experiences teach wonderful lessons, and they refuse to use or accept the lesson which the broader experiences of their parents have taught them.

The freedom and independence in this country bring the children into conflict with their parents. They learn nicer ways, learn about the outside world, learn how to speak English, and then they become ashamed of their parents who brought them up here that they might have better advantages.[9]

Vigilance versus eloping is the constant story. Sometimes the girl goes to the extreme of allowing a young man sex freedom with her, in order that her mother will be forced to consent to a marriage. It would seem that more social distance problems arise in the Mexican immigrant's family because of the conflict between Mexican and American customs than for any other reason.

The parents, however, are usually forgiving and take the young couple "back home." Occasionally, the girl is forced to go and live with her husband in his family group. These early marriages often mean numerous children, continued poverty, early aging, over-congestion in housing conditions, and other problems.

Oh, I must tell you, they have a bride and groom living there now. It was all an elopement that happened while I was away. You know Mexican parents are very careful about letting their daughters go places. They are much more particular than American parents are, I think. They never are allowed to go places unchaperoned, and the girls expect this, too.

Well, this little girl ran away and got married to her friend, G. She was in the right, too. She was sixteen and really old enough to be married as the Mexican age goes. But her mother just watched her all the time, never let her out of her sight, not even in the yard or house. But one day, oh yes, this girl had it all planned out, she was in her mother's bedroom and waved out

_____
9 From interview materials submitted by A. E. M.

the window to her friend who was standing in his yard, down the road. He hastened up to the girl's house, put his arm out, and she rushed out the door, put her arm in his, and away they went—in his car that was drawn up at the roadside. They were married at S—; her people didn't like it much, but there they are.[10]

The problems of the migratory Mexican family are in part the result of labor conditions in the United States. Particularly in the Southwest is the Mexican family likely to move a number of times annually. Housing conditions among migratory families are often unsanitary. The temporary stay in any given locality means that only the cheapest of housing facilities are usually obtained.

Intermarriages between Mexican immigrants and the members of other races, sometimes take place on a low culture level. Ignorant Mexicans marry low-grade Negros, Japanese, Filipinos, and Europeans or Americans; higher-level interracial marriages also occur. In all cases, the biological problems of amalgamation are relatively unimportant. Data are incomplete, but on the whole the children of such mixed marriages do not give evidence of being particularly different from the children of intra-racial parents on corresponding culture levels. The real problem comes from the conflict of the different cultures represented. The contracting parties to such marriages clash because of culture differences and of resultant misunderstandings. More serious still are the attitudes of the relatives and friends of the contracting parties. Each of the latter is likely to be ostracized by the relatives and friends of the other party. Life is thus made miserable through loss of status. Some intermarriages, however, turn out well. The following excerpt represents a successful intermarriage.

One day an American man, oh, so handsome, came into the store. He was a shoe man from some other place. I saw him and I liked his looks right away. He did not pay any attention to me, but in one more week he came back, and I saw him again. Each week he came back. We got acquainted soon, and do you know, I fell in love with him and now he is my husband. He is such a good man. Oh, he is so nice with me. We are so happy together, and you know my sister in A—, her husband manages a shoe store there. She met him because he was a friend of my husband.

---

[10] From interview materials submitted by G. A. S.

I wish my F. liked good music like I love good music. We do not go to the concerts any more. F. is always so tired, and many times he has to work. I miss the good music but we have a Victrola and I play the records all day. See the many records. (She showed me the records with much interest. We discussed the various pieces, and I noticed her collection was one of the best that could be imagined. Her records were carefully chosen, and they represented the best of music and the best of artists.)

You know I still have trouble with my English. I heard somebody say one day, "dumb-bell." I thought it was a lovely name, so at noon I fixed a very good lunch, and when my husband came home I went to the door to meet him and kiss him like I always do, and I said, "Hello, dumb-bell." And he said, "N., what is this you call me, dumb-bell? What do you call me dumb-bell for, don't you love me?" He looks so cross with me, and I said, "F. what is the matter? Dumb-bell is a nice name." "No, dumb-bell is a bad name, don't ever call anybody dumb-bell, it is a bad name." Oh, I was so sorry I could not eat my lunch. I love my husband so much and I called him a bad name. Tell me, was it wrong to ask my neighbor what is a dumb-bell?"[11]

In a study of home ownership, a number of reasons why Mexican immigrants respond even to limited opportunities have been compiled. These reasons are drawn directly from interviews with Mexicans and reveal the practical as well as the human nature quality of these interesting people. Home owners gave eight main reasons for buying:

1. For the sense of security. A landlord cannot put them out for not being able to pay rent. Those who sell to Mexicans are more lenient about payments. The reason is evident.

2. It is easier to buy than to rent. It costs less. They must pay $20 or $25 a month if they rent. They can buy for $10 a month.

3. It is difficult to rent with children. They tell the story of hunting for houses and then being compelled to move into a shack because they have children.

4. They have better homes when they own them. Furniture is nicer. It isn't scratched in moving.

5. To save the trouble of moving.

6. Not to be bothered by the landlord "snooping" around to see if the children have spoiled anything. What the children do to the house is nobody's business but your own, when you own it.

7. So that the chldren will have a place to play unmolested.

8. So that the home will be paid for when the children are grown. This will allow for more money with which to provide advantages for the children.[12]

---

[11] From interview materials submitted by H. W. W.
[12] From interview materials submitted by B. M. F.

With the coming of the depression in the fall of 1929 this development has been changed. Homes partly paid for have had to be given up, and worse still, in many cases the Mexicans have lost all the equity. Many have returned or been sent back to Mexico, being forced to lose all that they had put into homes.

In considering the budgets of "100 Mexican non-migratory, wage-earning families residing in a Mexican neighborhood in 1929-1930" in San Diego, Dr. Constantine Panunzio shows that the average annual total expenditure was $1,382.68 (or $45.33 more than the average income for the same group of people). The average amount spent for food was $506.58 or 36.6 per cent; for clothing, $188.50; and for housing (98 families), $225.57.[13] The food includes chiefly corn, beans, and fats. While the food is Mexican, the clothing is adopted, including "overalls, wool suits, ready-made dresses, silk stockings." Housing is found in separate, detached, one-family dwellings in nearly two thirds of the cases.[14]

Again, we have a situation which has been changed by the depression. As income has decreased, food has claimed an increasing percentage of it. Family life, however, among the Mexicans has maintained itself remarkably well. While the spiritual ties of family life have been strained, they have generally held even when the material resources have disappeared.

---

[13] Constantine Panunzio, *How Mexicans Earn and Live* (Berkeley: University of California Publications in Economics, 1933), p. 29.

[14] *Ibid.*, pp. 32, 37, 40.

CHAPTER IV

HEALTH AND HYGIENE

Health conditions in Mexican communities and camps are on the whole far from satisfactory. The average Mexican immigrant has not been accustomed to sanitation and hygiene. He has been uninstructed. The law of the survival of the fittest has operated. High mortality rates, especially among the young children, have prevailed. Health attitudes are in process of development.

Unfavorable climatic conditions in certain sections of Mexico, inadequate food, and a dull social life have combined to make "a lazy Mexican." Tuberculosis is one of the Mexican's deadliest enemies, and undernourishment is widespread. Doctors are either shunned or unknown; hospitals are feared.

Mexican immigrant women sometimes wash clothes every day, and generally have clothes hanging on a line, a fence, or on bushes. Many Mexican peons, however, neglect to keep their bodies clean. Stereotypes have unfortunately developed in the minds of many Americans, until they think of Mexicans as dirty and unclean; and they recoil. They object to the presence of Mexican children in the schools that their children attend, for fear that the latter will catch a contagious disease. A relatively permanent form of racial antipathy is the result.

The unhealthful and unsanitary conditions of many Mexican communities are due in part to the irresponsible attitudes that people of the United States take toward Mexicans. There are numerous income-producing properties, occupied by Mexicans but owned by citizens of the United States in good standing, which are tuberculosis-infected. They are allowed to continue in their illness-producing and death-dealing rôles, because love of money by some "Americans" is greater than love of the Mexican's health and life, and because the public is ignorant and careless regarding the dangers of slums to the occupants. These properties are generally in transition areas, that is, in areas that were once residential but are becoming industrial and business districts. Hence, it does not pay the individual owners to put and keep them in decent living shape. Thus, Mexican immigrants often are victims not only of their own ignorance but also of "American" greed, carelessness, and ignorance.

When faced with the charge that they allow the Mexicans' quarters to remain unfit for respectable living, some people in the United States reply that such quarters while unsatisfactory are nevertheless better than the Mexicans were accustomed to in Mexico, and that the latter would not appreciate better conditions. This comment would apply to certain Mexicans, as it would also to certain members of every race, but it does not accurately represent all Mexicans. "American" employers are oftentimes grossly negligent regarding the health and welfare of their migratory workers; they forget that the sum total of the temporary periods of work constitute the Mexican's permanent year. Thus the uneducated Mexican falls into abysses of illness and death between the irresponsibility of employers and of the public.

Of the 12,119 patients cared for by the Los Angeles County Health Department for the fiscal year ending June 30, 1933; 4,440 cases or 36.7 per cent were Mexican; and of the 17,677 patients of the Maternal and Child Hygiene Conferences, 4,231 cases or 23.9 per cent were Mexican. These percentages are much higher than the percentage of Mexicans in the total population of the County; they also show that Mexicans are responding extensively to health facilities.[1]

A splendid health movement in behalf of Mexicans is being developed. County and city health officials, and the public schools in Mexican districts are doing fine pieces of work. On the whole when the health workers gain the confidence of the Mexicans, the latter respond well. Of course, the Mexican sometimes remonstrates, due to superstitious elements in his culture. In Huerfano County, Colorado, a school nurse reports the case of a father who protested against having his daughter's heavily matted and uncombed hair cut because "if you cut off her hair, she will lose all her strength and surely die."[2] Another

---

[1] From data furnished by the Los Angeles County Health Department.

[2] R. N. McLean and Charles A. Thomson, "Spanish and Mexican in Colorado," Board of National Missions, Presbyterian Church in the U.S.A., New York, 1924, p. 11.

illustration is that of the father who objected to having antitoxin given his child who was ill with diphtheria, because he
feared that the antitoxin would kill the child. The problem is
not peculiar to Mexicans; it exists wherever attempts are made
to improve the health conditions of any uneducated people.

Health provisions cost Mexicans relatively a small amount,
due in part to the free aid which they receive, and in part to
their simple standard of living. In a study of 100 Mexican
families in San Diego in 1929-1930, Dr. Constantine Panunzio
found that seventeen families received no medical attention
whatever during the year under study, that ten were cared for
free of charge, that fifty-three paid a part of the costs, and
that twenty were entirely self-sustaining.[3] In the case of the
twenty who paid for all their own medical needs, the cost for
the year ranged from three dollars to eighty-two dollars, or
an average of $31.76. For the fifty-three families that paid
in part for their medical needs the total average cost was $41.81
for the year.

Under stimulating home teachers, conditions show marked
improvement. A social worker in what was once an ill-kept
Mexican camp testifies to what may take place under sanitary
guidance.

When the Mexicans first located there, they were pretty dirty. But
they are a lot better now. Their houses are kept better and their yards are
more attractive. They are much cleaner. Of course, their ways of doing
things are different from ours. They scrub their houses up differently than
we do. But we expect that.[4]

The excerpt that follows refers to one of the lowest grades
of Mexican camps. A community nurse reveals some of the
prevalent attitudes.

Yes, we help the Mexicans some, through our clinic. I go down there
one day a week to their camp and hold a clinic for babies. The women come
with their babies and I weigh them and give them advice. They don't
think much of that, though. They have their own ways of doing things.
They don't like to bring them to me, except when they're sick. If their
small children are ailing, they bring them along, too.[5]

---

[3] Constantine Panunzio, *How Mexicans Earn and Live* (Berkeley: University of California Publications in Economics, 1933), p. 58.

[4] E. S. Bogardus, "The Mexican Immigrant," *Journal of Applied Sociology,* 11: 486.

[5] From interview materials submitted by G. A. S.

One of the last traits to be changed of a people who have migrated is the food pattern. The Mexicans run true to form in this regard, but even here changes may be expected in the case of the second generation. The second excerpt that follows indicates how Mexicans change even with reference to tenacious food habits.

I don't try to change their diet much. The babies eat things we Americans couldn't stand but they are used to it and seem to thrive on it. They would get puny on our American food. Really though, their food is nourishing. Their beans are lots better for them than some of our rich American food would be.[6]

A change has come about in their food. The Mexican enjoys highly seasoned food and plenty of chili. The Mexican children are beginning to desire American food, little or no chili, and a substitute of flour for meal. One woman said: "My husband sings in Hollywood. He eats American food there all the time. He comes home every Sunday. He says he gets tired of American food and wants Mexican food. He likes much chili. I make tamales for my boys with no chili. They don't like it. They like American food best.[7]

No one can see the women of the lower classes in Mexico engaged in washing clothes on stones by a river and not realize that here is a real desire for that cleanliness that is next to godliness. With adequate childhood backgrounds and later training in hygiene and sanitation the Mexican peon as a class responds as well to satisfactory standards as do any people of similar culture levels.

---

[6] *Ibid.*

[7] From interview materials submitted by C. G. S.

CHAPTER V

LABOR AND INDUSTRY

The occupations which the Mexican immigrants have entered are, first of all, agricultural. Raising and picking cotton, the beet industry, the cultivation of lettuce, walnuts, oranges and lemons, grapes, cantaloupes, and a large number of similar activities are representative.[1]

In a normal year the Mexicans pick oranges from January to March, cultivate cantaloupes in February and March, pick cantaloupes from May to August, pick Valencias from April to July, pick grapes in September and October, chop and thin lettuce in the fall months, harvest peas in October and other months, and so on throughout a long list of diversified activities.

Unfortunately these fruits grow in zones in the United States and the Mexican must migrate from one region to another with the changing months. The demand for migratory labor has been strong; the resultant social problems are many. A migrant labor class is inimical to stable social order.

If migratory agricultural workers constitute one class of Mexican immigrants, then a second classification includes the Mexicans who have "settled down" on ranches or in small camps. Even these, however, are sometimes subject to migration. They are also the victims of changing economic conditions.

Many are employed steadily on diversified large-scale ranches; others work for small-scale ranchers where only one or two or a half dozen laborers are needed. Such ranchers run the gamut of human types.

In the third place there are the railroad workers. Many of these live in box cars and are continually on the move. Others reside in railroad company houses "along the tracks" and work in the "yards" or on the "roads." Congestion and other untoward housing conditions exist.

---

[1] In California alone it is estimated that there are 160 different crops in which Mexican labor is employed.

A large fourth group are the unskilled Mexican laborers in the cities; they are engaged in a wide range of activities, such as street improvement work (employed extensively by the public utility companies), and excavation work (for new houses and other buildings). They congregate at certain centers, sometimes on given street corners, to which employers come whenever they want "a hand" or any number of unskilled laborers. Work, thus, is irregular.

There may also be noted, fifth, the Mexican skilled laborer, living in cities. A number of Mexicans is found in the skilled trades, such as carpentry, painting, plumbing, and masonry. The opportunities are not numerous. Another difficulty is the attitudes of those "Americans" who believe that "once a Mexican, always a Mexican," which means that the Mexican has few chances of advancement. There are people who insist on thinking that the Mexican is unable to rise above an unskilled labor level. They cannot visualize a Mexican immigrant on any other plane. This widespread type of thinking is an actual hindrance to the Mexican's advancement. Many Mexicans are skilled along special lines, such as woodcarving, but again, opportunities are scarce.

A sixth occupational type is the Mexican in business. Mexican business men operate small stores in Mexican communities. The numbers are significant, and the type of business is not dissimilar to that found among small storekeepers anywhere. The man and his wife often operate the business together. Some Mexicans are contractors; a few operate a small chain of stores. They cater chiefly to the elemental wants of their own people; hence, the stimuli to develop are not exciting.

The professional group, a seventh classification, is not to be ignored. Small in numbers, they are able to eke out only a fair living at best. Some are artists and musicians, with little chance for recognition. An occasional girl becomes "a movie star." Some are ministers, especially in the Protestant denominations. A few are lawyers and doctors, whose services are limited to their own people. In the professional groups are found persons of superior ability to whom chances for advancement are few. Some American motion picture companies have given opportunities to Mexicans to come to Hollywood and a few individuals have become stars.

The incentives to Mexicans to immigrate to the United States have been chiefly economic. The higher wages have been effective stimuli. Three dollars a day, for instance, in 1929, looked large to a Mexican accustomed to receiving the equivalent of fifty cents. Six or eight pesos a day looked "like a million dollars." Relatively stable political conditions in the United States appeal to Mexicans who have grown tired of revolutions. As stability has developed in Mexico and economic opportunities have declined in the United States, immigration has naturally decreased.

Agents of large-scale American employers have crossed the Border and made glowing statements about the labor demands and the high wages in the United States. Whole groups of Mexicans have been contracted for and all expenses of transportation to places of work in the United States have been paid. When the Mexican's labor is no longer wanted, he has been left to drift back as best he may. The higher wages, but not the higher cost of living in the United States, have been emphasized. The Mexican thinks of "six pesos in terms of living expenses in Mexico." Indirectly, thus, inflated promises are made to Mexicans. Some agents are credited with having painted glowing word pictures of what is done for the Mexican immigrant, and of totally ignoring what is not done for him. The urgent demands for labor but not its seasonal and irregular character have been described.

In presenting the data for one hundred non-migratory, Mexican, wage-earners' families for the year 1929-1930 in San Diego, Dr. Panunzio shows that the average income per family per year was $1,337.35 and that the average amount earned by the husband (in 98 cases) was $1,085.41; that the wives' average earnings (in 43 cases) was $276.50; while the children earned $502.71 per family (in 16 families).[2] How these figures contrast with the scanty income of the more recent days of depression and unemployment is not difficult to visualize.

The wage problem has a number of interesting angles. While wages in the United States have been two or three times as high as in Mexico, the cost of living is likewise higher and

---

[2] Constantine Panunzio, *How Mexicans Earn and Live* (Berkeley: University of California Publications in Economics, 1933), pp. 14, 15.

the irregularity of work is great. A three dollar wage per day has often meant an income of not more than six or seven hundred dollars a year, even for the hard-working, ambitious Mexican, because of the uncertainties of day labor. This sum, however, is meager when one considers the needs of a family totaling five, six, or seven, trying to attain to American standards.

Another angle to the higher wage situation is that the Mexican peon immigrant is not trained to save. In Mexico he did not have enough income to meet the necessities of life. There was nothing for him to save. Saving is a foreign concept to him. His higher wage in the United States, therefore, is something to be spent—usually at the end of the week that it is earned. Unfortunately, there are both "Americans" and fellow Mexicans on hand not only to help him spend his larger earnings, but to help him spend it wastefully. Omnipresent advertising, widespread example, alluring appeals steal away the higher wages.

The *labor contract system* has worked grave injustices to the Mexicans. According to it the agriculturist arranges with a labor contractor to perform a certain extensive piece of work, for example, in the harvesting of a given crop. Labor contractors may bid against each other and must make some profit, and hence the laborer's wage is pushed down. Moreover, the laborer loses direct contact with his farmer-employer, and the latter fails to assume responsibility for the untoward conditions under which the Mexican works. Another evil arises from the fact that the agriculturist retains perhaps twenty-five per cent of the contract price until the entire labor job is satisfactorily completed. Hence, the contractor holds back one fourth of the wages due to the laborers until the completion of the contract, and then sometimes "skips out," leaving the Mexicans unpaid for one fourth of their work.[3]

Likewise, the *family contract system of labor* is also harmful. The harvesting of sugar beets, for example, in Colorado is paid for by the ton. The amount paid is so inadequate that the father must call upon his whole family to help him. The

3 *Mexicans in California.* Report of Governor C. C. Young's Mexican Fact-Finding Committee, San Francisco, 1930, pp. 130 ff.

wife is taken out of the home and the children out of school. Again the agriculturist stands off remotely and disclaims any responsibility for child labor, truancy from school, and the like, which the system engenders. Moreover, the Mexican father is the one who is charged with being a law breaker and a heartless opponent of compulsory education for his children.

The real development of labor unions among Mexican workers in southern California began in 1927. An initial convention of the Confederation of Mexican Labor Unions was held in Los Angeles, May 5-7, 1928.[4] Delegates came from twenty-three labor organizations and represented nearly all of the southern portion of the state. The movement seems to have originated in a sense of injustice concerning working conditions.

In the spring of 1928 the labor union movement began to make itself felt, for a strike of Mexican cantaloupe pickers took place in Imperial Valley, California, which attracted statewide attention.[5] The strike was a protest of Mexican workers against the alleged unfairness of the labor contractors representing the employers.[6]

This labor union movement died down until the summer and fall of 1933, when several strikes were staged by Mexicans. For example, in June, 1933, it is claimed that a total of several thousands of Mexicans went on strike in southern California alone. One of the strikes centered in El Monte, California, where Mexican laborers went on strike against the Japanese for whom they were working as berry pickers. The race factor seems to have been negligible. Three other elements in the situation, however, were important. First, there were the low wages paid the Mexicans; these were reported to be as low as nine cents an hour. Second, there was the influence of Communist agitators who by the use of speakers and mimeographed dodgers stirred up the Mexicans to strike for better wages. Third, there was a new Mexican labor union movement among the Mexican laborers that developed in 1933 and was known as the *Confederacion de Uniones de Campesinos y*

---

[4] *Ibid.*, p. 126.

[5] *Ibid.*, p. 135.

[6] The strikers were arrested and later released. Labor contracts were revised to the advantage of the workers.

Obreros Mexicanos del Estado de California, or the *CUCOM,*
which was reported to hold a charter from the *Confederacion
Regional de Obreros Mexicanos (CROM)* and to be viewed
favorably by representatives of the American Federation of
Labor. The labor strike at El Monte, which was temporarily
settled on July 6, 1933, by an agreement fixing a minimum
wage for Mexican farm workers at twenty cents an hour, is
somewhat representative of other recent strikes in which Mexican laborers have figured.[7]

The Mexican peon, as a whole, does not organize well. Like
other unskilled laborers, he does not appreciate the advantages
of labor unions. He is not educated to the level of unionization.
Union men say that the Mexican "works so cheaply that no
white man can compete with him." Under migratory and seasonal labor conditions, the Mexican does not stay in one place
long enough to be organized. That he is capable of unionization is shown by the Mexican labor union movement in the
United States and the strong growth of labor unions in Mexico.
With education and training, he may become effective as a
unionist.

Organized labor both in the United States and in Mexico is
resentful of immigration from Mexico. The attitudes of organized labor in Mexico are to be explained by the real and alleged exploitation of Mexican immigrants in the United States.
The reactions of organized labor in the United States are due
to the potential competition which the Mexican laborer offers,
that is, to the belief that Mexican labor "keeps down" labor
standards. In 1927, the American Federation of Labor inaugurated a policy of favoring quota restrictions. Attempts have
been made whereby the American Federation and the Mexican
Federation might work out a plan of restriction that could be
put into effect in both countries.

In gold mining and lumber camp regions of the Southwest
and the Northwest the I.W.W. has numbered Mexicans in its
ranks. In the lumber camps, I.W.W. organizers have been able
to make a considerable appeal to dissatisfied Mexicans. Simi-
larly in mining, the I.W.W. organizer finds that degree of dis-

---

[7] For a more detailed statement of the El Monte strike see article on
"The Mexican Strike in El Monte" by Charles B. Spaulding, appearing in
Sociology and Social Research, XVIII:571-80, July-August, 1934.

satisfaction which enables him to develop a following. Unfavorable living and working conditions, including "hard-boiled bosses," often account for the dissatisfaction on which the I.W.W. thrives.

Unskilled Mexicans as a class require supervision. Without some one directing them, they are likely to take time off freely. They live so largely in the present that time has no particular meaning to them. With them time is not commercialized as with us. Their wants ordinarily are not aroused as are ours, and consequently they do not drive themselves as we drive ourselves.

There is little or no opportunity for wholesome contacts between Mexican laborers and their large-scale employers. The boss, as the immediate supervisor, is expected to secure a certain amount of labor from the Mexicans as cheaply as possible. Many employers in the United States treat the Mexicans "like dogs"; others trust them and are trusted in turn. A few assume some responsibility for the culture development of the Mexicans.

We may now consider briefly the labor conditions of Mexican girls and women. Numbers are employed in citrus packing, in walnut picking, and similar work. Not many are employed as household help, because they lack the necessary knowledge and training. However, the number who are going into homes as workers by the day or hour is slowly increasing, but they are handicapped because of their lack of knowledge of English and of American household methods.

Social welfare agencies are trying to secure places in homes in the United States for Mexican girls and women as employees. A social worker states:

Americans want household help for two or three days a week, and they can, if they will, take Mexican women and teach them. It requires patience to be sure, but there are large numbers of Mexicans who can fill the household gap if the proper connections are made.

A representative of a social settlement reports: "We could keep one person busy for full time in this form of employment adjustment."

Take the case of a Mexican girl who is employed in a small department store to wait on the Mexican trade. Upon being interviewed, the forelady said:

Oh yes, we are all very fond of Miss H. She is quiet and refined. She certainly is of great assistance here. She speaks Spanish very well and understands the needs and wants of the Mexicans. Miss H. used to be in the notion department, but recently has been promoted to the hosiery department.[8]

A considerable number of Mexican women are teachers in the public schools—as many as forty in one urban community alone. Others are taking nurses' training. Numbers are employed in Mexican stores or American stores needing Mexican saleswomen. Some are becoming business women and are operating small stores and the like.

A few of the problems confronting Mexican men as laborers will now be considered. The questions have often been raised: Cannot American needs for Mexican labor be distributed throughout the year, and cannot migratory labor be made unnecessary? There is agricultural work, for example, in the Southwest for every month in the year. However, many of the crops which need attention in successive seasons are located in areas remote from each other. In a given region, there are two, three, or more months of the year when special agricultural labor demands are low or nil. Hence the choice is between remaining idle a part of the year or of migrating many miles annually. Even in migrating there is much lost motion. Observers on the Ridge Route, California, have found two streams of Mexicans immigrants—one going north, the other south, at the same time of the year. Despite the belief of many employers that "it is impossible to colonize permanent labor in the various towns and give them year around employment," the evidence to this end is by no means conclusive. No real, large-scale attempt at equalization of labor needs has been made to date.

A clearing-house program has been strongly advocated, whereby unemployed Mexicans and unoccupied jobs might be brought together. Mexicans are needed in certain rural districts at certain seasons; Mexicans are unemployed and seeking work at the same time in urban centers. A sort of directing arm has been suggested which would move the Mexicans here and there, when and where they are needed. The employers

---

8 From interview materials submitted by G. A. S.

would gain, but what about the total welfare of the employee? The Mexican has often been made a kind of labor tramp; the proposed adjustment plan would not solve but would speed up the undesirable labor tramp tendency. Transient labor with many of its gross defects would be increased instead of being eliminated. Migratoriness creates unrest, makes home life difficult, hinders the proper education of children, and arrests the growth of constructive citizenship.

A more fundamental type of adjustment that is needed would be for agriculture to diversify and to establish permanent living conditions, to develop the home life and the education of children in districts where now only migratory seasonal labor demands obtain. There is a need to transform the present undiversified but seasonal labor districts into regions affording diversified and all-year labor opportunities, home ownership, standard education facilities, and a permanent outlook on life for Mexicans and everyone else who may wish to accept.

Experiences in Germany with contract labor from Czechoslovakia or in France with contract labor from Italy are cited in support of the proposal to bring immigrants in from Mexico for six months at a time under government supervision. European conditions, however, are different from American; Germans and Czechoslovakians (with their German connections) possess similar culture traits; French and Italians are in many ways similar. But the people of the United States and the Mexicans are widely different in culture and racial traits. The wider the differences between two peoples the greater is the likelihood that a contract labor system will create grave evils.

It is probable, with the improvement of economic conditions in Mexico and with Mexico keeping close watch over emigration, that the present Mexican immigrant situation in the United States will improve. If Mexican laborers in the United States permanently decrease, more care will be given to them by their employers in the United States. Diversification of industry in given regions in the United States will tend to create permanent living conditions for Mexicans. With both working and living conditions on the mend and with government control on the increase, a solution of some of the worst phases of the Mexican immigrant problem may be at hand.

CHAPTER VI

PROPERTY AND POVERTY

The Mexican peon is hacienda-minded. He has not been trained in assuming responsibility. He has not had much of this world's goods for which to become responsible. He has not been taught to save; he has had little or nothing to save. Thrift has not entered his vocabulary. Poverty has been his natural lot.

The Mexican peon is stimulated to come to the United States chiefly by the reports of high wages. He comes to work, to get "beeg money," and to spend. He works with the idea of frequently taking a few days off in order to enjoy the fruits of his labor.

Employers have given him work in prosperous times and then have discarded him without warning in harsh times. As a rule the people who have induced him to come assume no responsibility for his welfare as soon as his labor is no longer needed.

Large employer organizations have no expense connected with the Mexican immigrant after he leaves their employ. They do not wish any. They refuse to take any responsibility in the matter. The Mexican is junked, just like an old machine, when most convenient to the employer, with the full knowledge that when help is again needed it will be forthcoming. This is to me little better than slavery. The slave owner was obliged to care for the slaves during idle times and during illness, because they cost him money. Not so with the employer who uses the Mexican immigrant laborer. When he is no longer able to carry a spade, the assumption seems to be that he no longer needs food. The responsibility is shifted to someone else, the charity organizations, for instance; that work belongs to them.[1]

In the United States, moreover, the Mexican hears no more about thrift than in Mexico; he is surrounded with a spending psychology. Life is pitched high, industrial activities are impersonal, a harsh individualistic philosophy predominates. *Mañana,* which is a survival concept in Mexico, is fatal in the United States. Not everything can be put off until tomorrow;

---

[1] From interview materials submitted by E. H. M.

tomorrow does not always or usually take care of itself. Furthermore, tomorrow often comes swiftly and relentlessly.

However, the *mañana* spirit is a plea for the enjoyment of the present, and a protest against a hectic machine age. It is a protest against ever rushing here and yon, grasping after a few strains of minor pleasures when greater pleasure can be had close at hand, in fact, from within one's own soul. It is a protest against a jazzed-up age controlled by a speed demon. It may be that the much-maligned *mañana* spirit of the Mexican represents an excellent antidote to the evils of a grasping, motor-driven, neurasthenic race for economic power. Under certain circumstances it may represent a superior philosophy of life.

In Mexico, the peon's customs include gambling. In the United States, the high wages are special excitants of gambling. Fellow Mexicans and even "Americans" are unscrupulous enough to appeal to the human tendency to take chances, and hence are partly responsible for the Mexican immigrant's poverty.

The general opinion, however, that all Mexican immigrants are hopelessly thriftless is not borne out by the facts which show how much money is sent back via money orders to Mexico. These figures as presented by Manuel Gamio are amazing. If they could have as much publicity as are given the reports concerning the Mexican's thriftlessness, the American public would have a new stereotype of the Mexican immigrant. Of course, it is true that numbers of Mexican immigrants, like members of other races, might profit by a training in thrift. "You need to put the Scotchman into the Mexican." The figures in terms of pesos sent to Mexico by Mexican immigrants for seven prosperity years by money orders alone are given by Dr. Gamio[2] as stated in Table IV on the following page.

Although the poverty of the unskilled Mexican is high in Mexico, he has not been accustomed to ask for public aid. He had received a great deal of assistance in a communal spirit from his kin, friends, and hacienda owners. His is a communal-spirit background rather than an individualistic and public-aid background.

----

2 Manuel Gamio, *Mexican Immigration to the United States* (Chicago: University of Chicago Press, 1930), p. 5.

TABLE IV

PESOS SENT TO MEXICO BY MEXICAN IMMIGRANTS
VIA MONEY ORDERS

Year	Pesos
1921	4,508,867.89
1922	6,465,485.26
1923	16,013,475.70
1924	10,752,482.58
1925	9,950,131.16
1926	13,307,046.15
1927	16,630,189.48

He brings his poverty with him, confronts a long period of adjustment here, and finds that his total annual income measures low against American purchasing prices. It is not surprising to learn that his poverty rate is somewhat higher than his population rate. His poverty rate, however, is not so high as popular opinion would lead one to believe. According to a report from the Department of Public Welfare of the County of Los Angeles for the year ending December 31, 1933, the Mexican represents 11.7 per cent of the total case load, which is but little higher than his estimated proportion of 8 to 10 per cent of the county's population.[3]

When the Mexican peon with his paternalistic and communal culture has come into contact with American individualism, he has tottered. When he has been encouraged to migrate in larger numbers than labor needs require, he has fallen into harsh paths. When he has become the victim of migratory labor conditions, his economic progress has been balked. When he has attempted to acquire real estate, the total costs and the adverse prejudices have been forbidding. When he has been taken advantage of in this country by both "Americans" and fellow Mexicans, he has become confused and discouraged.

The Mexican immigrant has been and still is the victim of a Christmas basket paternalism. A Christmas basket for one day in the year and poverty for 364 days is poor philanthropy. It has been described as a tip to keep the Mexican from becoming a bolshevist. Industrial adjustment involving an economic self-sufficiency for all the year, so that the Mexican could buy his own Christmas baskets, is the real need.

---

[3] On March 15, 1934, the Mexican cases in Los Angeles County were reported as 10.8 per cent of the whole.

The Mexican has often been pauperized by cheap publicity methods of philanthropy. In effect, he has been taught to look for gratuities, and he has been dissatisfied if he did not receive as good a dole as he expected. He has even been known to secure several Christmas baskets at the same Christmas season from different kind-hearted organizations.

Improved attitudes are developing. Welfare agencies are using the confidential exchange and avoiding duplication. They are making scientific case studies and employing social workers who can help in the problems of personal and family reorganization, so that individuals and families may become self-supporting. Social welfare agencies would like to increase the proportion of their budgets for rehabilitation work and decrease the proportion for groceries and rents. Even business men, county supervisors, are beginning to see the value of personnel work among the Mexicans and the weakness of a grocery and rent philanthropy.

Not charity but a chance for the Mexican, has been a slogan of the Goodwill Industries in the Southwest. By this organization the handicapped Mexican or members of the Mexican family who are unemployed, are given work and in the meantime trained for something better; they are helped through work and training to get on their feet and to go ahead under their own initiative to better jobs.

The problems of industrial and social reorganization remain to be solved. No amount of personal reorganization work can help any one to become self-sufficient if economic and social conditions are disorganizing. Distribution of labor opportunities throughout the year, together with distribution of laborers and their families where they are needed, and where they can live permanently, are essential minima. Such a procedure will make so-called welfare work unnecessary; it is real welfare-work.

The charity rate, as judged by county departments of charity, remains high for Mexican peons even when they have been here ten years or longer. This fact may be interpreted in a number of ways: (1) that the opportunities to work are irregular and that the chances for industrial advances for Mexicans are few; (2) that charity aid keeps them from assuming full economic initiative; and (3) that many are inherently lazy and shiftless. While all three of these factors probably are operative, it would appear that if the first could be properly adjusted, the second and third might largely take care of themselves.

The labor turnover problem revolves in a vicious circle. When a railroad reports a turnover of three hundred per cent in a single year, there must be something "rotten in Denmark." Either employer responsibility is almost nil, or the Mexicans are entirely undesirable. It is hard to understand how employers who insist on Mexican labor as being the most desirable labor that can be obtained should run excessive turnovers. It is natural, of course, that an employer does not want to spend money on training Mexicans to higher efficiency only to have them leave and seek employment elsewhere. And yet, how can the Mexican extricate himself from the turnover maelstrom? Poverty is a natural accompaniment of unskilled labor turnover. To cut down turnover would lessen poverty.

Ordinarily the Mexican does not come within the scope of the compensation and sickness insurance laws. Sometimes he is "bluffed out," and often he does not know that he is entitled to compensation or how to go about obtaining it. In case of sickness, he is doubly handicapped, for he loses his wages and his expenses increase.

A hopeful tendency is the increasing strength of Mexican benevolent societies. The Spanish-American Alliance alone has a large membership in southern California. The Blue Cross, the Mexican counterpart of the Red Cross, has developed in various communities of the Southwest. The Mexicans are beginning to organize to take care of their own needy.

Despite the high poverty rate and the reputation for financial irresponsibility, the Mexican as a class possesses the essential possibilities for financial responsibility and social independence. C. C. Teague, formerly of the Federal Farm Labor Board, is accredited with the statement that "it is doubtful if laborers of this class of any other nationality take care of their own people who become incapacitated and impoverished as well as do the Mexican people." Mr. Teague also referred to the high degree of willingness of even the poorest Mexicans to help each other, and to a large amount of simple personal service that is rendered the less fortunate by their neighbors and kin.

The Mexican peon arrives poor and he is not equipped to climb out of the slough of poverty. Conditions in the United States do not give him the proper stimuli or the essential opportunities for developing the necessary momentum. A sufficient number, however, have made the transition from a poverty to a property status, to demonstrate that the necessary changes can take place. For example, in V—, California, Mexicans were changing to a property and business level until the depression of 1929 came. Unfortunately such advancement arouses the prejudices of these "Americans" who are prone to criticize the Mexicans the loudest for being of a low cultural level.

Not long ago school bonds were voted for a grammar school for the first five grades of Mexicans. The Mexicans, however, were not content to remain on their previous level. They have now in the colony, two coöperative stores, two filling stations, a barber shop, and a shoe repairing shop. The V— merchants do not appreciate these signs of progress, but resent the considerable loss of trade that they have suffered, and think that the Mexicans are not sufficiently appreciative of what has been done for them.[3]

Give the Mexican a fair chance and he would become as self-sufficient as other people. Encourage him without prejudice to express himself and he might help to put materialism to rout, and do his part to create a new and better civilization.

---

[3] From interview materials submitted by E. H.

CHAPTER VII

CRIME AND DELINQUENCY

While the rank and file of Mexican immigrants have furnished an unusually high rate of crime and delinquency, there is no indication that they have any inherited tendencies of this nature that other races do not have. The abnormal rate can be accounted for on special environmental grounds, while the normal delinquency tendencies identify Mexicans with "Americans" and with all other peoples.

When Mexicans come from a land where customs are different from those in the United States it is both logical and natural that conflicts should arise and that certain "crimes" should result. Inasmuch as the peon, who has had little training in the meaning of private property concepts, finds himself in a country where private property is almost worshiped, he easily becomes guilty of stealing. His semi-communal backgrounds account in part for his tendency to pick up anything that interests him, to take it where he can enjoy it as long as it interests him, and then to throw it down without going through the formality of returning it to the particular place where he picked it up. He is somewhat like a small child brought up in a paternalistic home, who goes about the place freely, picking up and enjoying whatever touches his fancy.

The Mexican peon has a Latin sense of the attractive and the unattractive rather than the rigid and formal Anglo-Saxon sense of "rights." He is guided more by what appeals to his senses than by a complicated set of highly rationalized codes. He is a realist and opportunist, enjoying today as much as possible and putting all things else off until *mañana*, which may never come.

Crime statistics might be quoted to show that the unskilled Mexican immigrant ranks out of all proportion to his population numbers. The crime figures sometimes run from twenty to forty per cent of the total crimes committed in a community where his population numbers are only five or ten per cent of the total. It is unfair, however, to jump to the conclusion that the Mexican is two or three times as criminal as are other peoples, or that he is equally criminal in regard to all phases of life, or that all Mexicans are equally criminal. It is true that there are some Mexicans living under certain circumstances who "will steal everything that they can lay their hands on," but such a statement should be accompanied by another; namely, that there are other Mexicans who are as trustworthy and reliable as any human being. The good that many Mexican immigrants do is sometimes unsung; the evil that other Mexicans do is charged to the whole race and the generalization that is broadcast, "You can't trust a Mexican," is grossly misrepresentative and unfair.

The nature of the Mexican immigrant's crimes and the conditions under which they are committed are probably more significant than the ratios referred to in the foregoing paragraph. His crimes are usually elemental, simple, overt. Lack of self-control and of social control in a complex and perplexing environment are major explanations.

Aside from stealing, the offenses of Mexican peons are largely directed against each other. They reap the penalty of their own misdeeds. They are victims of uninhibited emotions. They rank abnormally high in crimes of personal violence against each other. They have brought their customs with them relative to settling their own disputes. These methods which are sometimes honorable in an elementary culture level, are "crimes" in our sophisticated civilization.

In Table V will be found the figures for the number of arrests of Mexicans in Los Angeles County for the fiscal year ending June 30, 1933. These arrests are classified by offenses and arranged in order of decreasing percentages of total offenses of all persons booked during the period in the County.[1] The Mexican population of the County of Los Angeles may be estimated at about 10 per cent of the total. Hence, the percentage of arrests of Mexicans considerably exceeds their population percentage. The largest total of offenses is due to drunk-

---

1 In the Report of the Police Department of the City of Los Angeles, for the calendar year ending December 31, 1933, Mexicans are cited 868 times, or 24.9 per cent of the total citations by races; and in a similar report from the Office of the Sheriff of Los Angeles County for the same period, Mexicans comprise 26.0 per cent of all the cases. See *Juvenile Research Bulletin*, Los Angeles, 2:3 (January-February, 1934).

enness. The drinking of liquor plays havoc with many of them, arousing passions beyond all control, leading to serious crimes, demoralizing an otherwise quiet and pleasant people.

TABLE V

ARRESTS OF MEXICANS, LOS ANGELES COUNTY
FISCAL YEAR ENDING JUNE 30, 1933[2]

Offense	No. of Arrests	Percentage of all Arrests Booked in County Jail
Violation State Poison Act	136	52.9
Disturbing Peace	153	35.7
Assault and Battery	168	28.2
Drunkenness	526	27.7
Violation Immigration Law	103	25.5
Murder	17	18.8
Rape, Other Sex Offenses	101	15.6
Violation Probation, Parole	17	14.9
Violation State Vehicle Act	270	14.8
Petty Theft	107	13.9
Failure to Provide	55	12.8
Grand Theft	162	12.2
Vagrancy	61	12.1
Burglary	157	12.0
Violation Liquor Laws	82	9.3
Arson	4	8.8
Forgery	17	2.6
Other and Unclassified	384	15.0
TOTAL	2552	15.1

An examination of the crimes of violence of Mexicans shows that these are distributed throughout all age groups, with a preponderance among those of middle age.[3] A parallel fact is that "this group of violators is not uniformly well educated." In general, "they come from the rank and file of the poorest paid laboring classes." Many cannot speak English. Large numbers are living in the United States but are not of it. Nothing has happened to many of them to arouse in them the desire to identify themselves with American life at its best.

---

[2] From mimeographed Report of Sheriff E. W. Biscailuz, County of Los Angeles, for fiscal year ending June 30, 1933.

[3] From a report by V. W. Killick, statistician and director of the Bureau of Public Relations, Los Angeles County Sheriff's Department, 1929 (a normal year).

Mariahuana is a native Mexican drug which causes havoc; it produces exhilaration and intoxication, "followed by extreme depression and broken nerves." Mariahuana is an enemy which follows many Mexicans to the United States, and which sometimes accounts for criminal acts. While under its influence, it is hard to tell how its victim will behave.

Vagrancy is a common charge against some Mexicans. As many as "twenty-six different sets of circumstances can be the basis of vagrancy charges" in the United States, hence, the term is used to cover a multitude of problems. Sometimes idleness and unemployment are sufficient to land a vagrancy charge on the Mexican's head. Lack of training and education, and lack of constructive opportunities account for the offenses of Mexicans. In these connections the Mexicans are strikingly similar to Americans or any other members of the human race. A study of crime among Mexicans identifies them as members of the human family. As Edward A. Steiner once said, "all members of the human race when taken at their best or at their worst are alike." [4]

Delinquency among juveniles centers around stealing, with burglary, grand larceny, motor vehicle act violations, probation and parole violations, and robbery, ranking high.[5] The records of a large state school for boys up to sixteen years of age show the following order of offenses for Mexican youth: (1) petty thieving, (2) automobile stealing, (3) morality offenses, and (4) truancy.

According to a statement from the Juvenile Probation Department of the County of Los Angeles, there was a total case load on March 1, 1934, of 3,974 boys and girls of school age, of whom 540 were Mexican or of Mexican parentage. In other words, these two groups of Mexican boys and girls comprised 13.5 per cent of the total. Four hundred thirty-five were Mexican boys or boys of Mexican parentage (14.9 per cent of all boys' cases). A total of 105 were Mexican girls or girls of Mexican parentage (9.8 per cent of all girls' cases).

---

[4] Edward A. Steiner, *Against the Current* (New York: Fleming H. Revell Company, 1910), p. 229.

[5] Based on reports for the fairly normal years of 1928 and 1929 by V. W. Killick, *op. cit.*

A social worker among Mexican immigrants has observed that children rebel most commonly against being suppressed by their parents. Children in the United States are allowed or take certain freedom. Mexican children long to do the same; they are suppressed; they become dissatisfied with their home life; sometimes they run away because they are required to help support the rest of the family when they want all their wages for themselves. This reaction is uncommon in Mexico; it develops in the United States as the result of the examples set by children in this country.

About one half of the cases handled by a given probation officer for Mexican boys are border-line or mentally defective. Their intelligence quotients range around 70. Only one in a group of 125 had an I. Q. over 105. The border-line for Mexican children is about ten points below that for other children in the United States, because of the language difficulty. The offenses which they commit as reported by a probation officer are: first, automobile and bicycle thefts; second, persistent truancy, to the extent where school officers cannot handle them; third, incorrigibility and running away from home; fourth, sex problems. The ages range from ten to eighteen with the mode at fourteen and fifteen.

The methods of treatment range from scientific case work to the traditional "bawling out" and the use of threats; they sometimes include appeals to the love for parents, picturing a crying mother to the boy if he should be sent to jail or a crying boy to the mother in case she is not willing to have the boy go to school or to coöperate in other ways. A constructive method is to provide playgrounds and to get boys to participate regularly on these playgrounds. At present, only a small percentage of the boys in many Mexican communities play regularly. Even where they attend a playground, troublesome problems still occur.

Training programs for parents are also being developed. In many instances, the parents are ignorant of child training methods. Very often the father will turn against his boy, and declare that if the boy has actually committed the reported offence, the father does not want the boy around. The officers spend some time in giving parental instruction. "Mexican peon parents have no ideas about raising children."

It is evident that many Mexican boys suffer all along the line. Their parents are at loss to meet their personality needs. Not all probation officers are up-to-date in their acquaintance with and practice in the latest and best case work methods; they are not equipped to deal adequately with difficult problems in personality reorganization. Their case loads are too heavy; the pay is too low to justify a probation officer in pursuing a technical training course. Supervisors and the public do not see the economy in securing well-trained workers to handle the personal disorganization and reorganization problems of Mexican boys and girls.

A probation officer for girls reports that a great many of the crimes committed by Mexican girls involve truancy and sex problems. The ages of these girls are between thirteen and seventeen years. Most of the trouble is due to ignorance of the law, poverty in the home, lack of sex education, and the fact that the father thinks the girls should begin while young to help support the family. The crowded conditions of the home are such that the girl must seek her pleasures elsewhere.

These and other factors are brought out in the various situations as described in court. Some of the Mexican girls run away from home to seek pleasure, and they are often afraid to return because of abuse and ill treatment at the hands of the fathers. One girl thirteen years old, for example, ran away and married a man of twenty-five. When asked why she married, her reply was, "I wanted to have nice clothes and a good time, and I couldn't have either at home."

Another case may be cited, namely, of a girl sixteen years old, whose father objected to having her go out with friends. When she disobeyed she was severely punished; then she would stay out at night because she was afraid to return home. She slept in parks or vacant lots rather than face the punishment that would be meted out by her father. The girl suffered disorganization and became a delinquent. The father finally had her placed in the House of the Good Shepherd.

It is surprising to observe how many Mexican girls find themselves in trouble and are brought into court when they have no intention of doing wrong. Many are like little children in an adult's environment. They have had little or no instruction in personality problems. They are little understood in their own homes, especially when they begin to follow the examples of other American girls. In becoming "American" they may become "delinquent." Urbanization leads them into situations where personal disorganization follows and where delinquency may be predicted.[6]

---

[6] Consult the study of the Russian Molokans of Los Angeles by Dr. Pauline V. Young, wherein it is shown how urbanization is a factor in delinquency among Russian immigrant children. The conflicts and problems seem to be racially universal. Pauline V. Young, *The Pilgrims of Russian Town* (Chicago: University of Chicago Press, 1932).

CHAPTER VIII

AMUSEMENTS AND MORALS

In Mexico the peon has no real recreation; neither do the lower classes in many countries. The peon, however, has a number of amusements, some of which are organized and institutionalized. Some are generators of serious vices. Gambling, cockfighting, the bullfight, talking, siestas, playing musical instruments, and dancing cover the list of major amusements.

While bullfighting "does not cross the Border," cockfighting bobs up here and there. Boxing and prize fighting receive considerable attention. Whenever Mexican boxers attract public interest, the younger Mexican generation grows wild with excitement. Boxing springs perennially into being in Mexican immigrant communities. Baseball and team games are still rather uncommon although receiving increasing attention. Both the Mexican's wish to be a leader and the migratory conditions of labor are hindrances to the growth of team games. The statement that every Mexican would like to be a general is of course a gross exaggeration, but it gives expression to a weakness that occasionally crops out when teamwork is attempted. The Mexican immigrant is fond of talking and "siestaing." While the drowsy climate of sections of his home country has had an influence, yet his lack of environmental stimuli and opportunities are doubtless the greater factors.

Dancing is a favorite amusement. Spanish and Mexican dances are immensely popular. The soul of the Mexican is oftentimes expressed better through dance than in any other way. The following lines paint a vivacious picture:

> A sudden tumult of wild melody,
> Then, shadow-like, athwart the terrace stair
> She darts, and pausing in the moonlight there,
> She flings her snapping castanets on high.
>
> We hear the music surge and softly die.
> O'er creamy arms a sea of ebon hair
> Falls rippling down where supple limbs are bare;
> A satin-slippered toe taps fretfully.

And then, we mark the rhyme of twinkling feet;
Beneath a turbaned brow chameleon eyes
Flash passioned star-flames 'mid the amber gloom.

As o'er us steals a languor strangely sweet,
And while the dreamy songs of maidens 'rise
We catch the floating breath of spiced perfume.[1]

The mandolin and guitar are omnipresent. Musical ability is common among Mexicans, but often it has remained untrained. As has been said of another race it is a pathetic sight to see a group of Mexicans "whiling away an afternoon in a jail to the tune of a guitar." American settlement and playground workers are here and there helping the Mexican to develop his musical talents. The public schools are doing much for Mexican children in music and pageantry. The Mexican at play is not distinguishable from the members of other races. He responds well to supervised encouragement.

The Mexican "takes" well to the national pastime of the United States, namely, baseball. More significant, through games such as baseball, he acquires a new meaning for teamwork.

Mexicans like all forms of ball-games. Sunday baseball and boxing are popular. They like the more brutal sports as wrestling, boxing, and tumbling. They will sit and crack knuckles just to see who can stand it the longest. Sometimes a boy will play a team game all by himself, but usually they coöperate well. They have learned this in school. Last year the Mexican clubs won eight city championships. Boys from eight to twenty years are taken into the clubs. They are divided into twelve and under, thirteen and fourteen, fifteen and sixteen, and over sixteen.[2]

When Mexicans attempt to join with people of the United States in their amusements, even to the extent of going to the latter's theaters, they are often affronted. So many people in the United States unfortunately generalize against all Mexicans on the basis of the lowest level Mexicans that the better class Mexicans grow discouraged and pessimistic regarding opportunities in the United States.

She went to a matinee show with an American friend of hers. This American girl is quite blond. S. is very light in complexion and would more

---

1 J. L. R. Burnett, "The Mexican Dancing Girl," *Outing*, 23:378.
2 From interview materials submitted by R. T. S.

easily pass for a French girl than a Mexican. The girls bought their tickets at the box, and when they went in, the ticket taker directed them upstairs. S. said, "These tickets are for downstairs." "I cannot help it; you are a Mexican and Mexicans sit upstairs." S. said, "Yes, I am a Mexican, and I am proud of it. I am with an American, and we are together; maybe she does not want to sit upstairs. I have been here many times before, and have always sat downstairs." The ticket taker said, "Don't talk to me about it; go talk to the woman at the box. I cannot do anything one way or another." S. returned to the ticket box, and discussed the matter with the ticket seller then. Her money was returned to her.[3]

Many a Mexican immigrant brings a lottery-mindedness.

This waiting for the lucky turn of the wheel is his curse. It deadens initiative, lessens the productive power of the individual, and lifting him out of the workaday present, sets him down in an illusive future built of the stuff of which dreams are made.[4]

Life is routine, but gambling adds excitement. The Mexican peon has little chance to get ahead by steady and enterprising activity; hence, he accepts the fleeting and uncertain gain that the lottery dangles before him.

True to the human type, the Mexican boys may form cliques, and may become "gangsters." As a member of a gang the Mexican often becomes disorganized and partly reorganized but not on broad lines. When constructive group life is afforded Mexican youth, they are not likely to become "moral menaces."

The Mexican's manners and morals are closely related. It is easy for him to say what he thinks is expected of him at the time. "The Mexican is so very courteous and gracious, that it is sometimes difficult to know what he really thinks, or what he really knows, or how he really feels," especially if he is talking with a stranger or visitor in his home.[5]

In morals, the Mexican immigrant as a class is not well organized to meet everyday problems in the United States. His simple life organization is no match for complex social conditions in the United States. To help the adult men and

---

[3] From interview materials submitted by H. W. W.

[4] R. N. McLean, *That Mexican* (New York: Fleming H. Revell and Company, 1928), pp. 33, 34.

[5] Helen W. Walker, "Mexican Immigrants and American Citizenship," *Sociology and Social Research*, 13:470.

women to become adequately reorganized is a stupendous task. Even the children are so greatly handicapped that their problems of personality organization require the highest type of social case work and teaching skill on the part of all who are interested.

CHAPTER IX

RELIGION AND ART

Mexicans are as religious as are other peoples. The Mexican immigrant has feelings and emotions which react readily to religious stimuli and become organized into religious sentiments. The peon comes with a simple childlike faith. The supernatural appeals to him forcefully. Dr. R. N. McLean portrays the Mexican's religious reactions as follows:

Suddenly across the still morning air, over the fields of corn and maguey, came floating like silvery music, the sound of the church bells. Soon men and women began to pass, walking with bare feet through the mud, to their priestless churches.

The current of the religious life of Juan Garcia has its source far back in the rugged mountains of his nation's history. Obstructions may stop it for a moment, but it cannot be restrained.

He hears the church bells ringing in his heart. His soul goes marching on.[1]

Migration is often a handicap to religious worship. Migratory labor conditions are especially disconcerting religiously. Like other peoples, Mexican immigrants do not keep up their religious practices in the customary ways, when away from home. The charge of being "nominally religious" is made against the Mexican immigrant, of keeping up religious forms and of observing certain holidays, but not of maintaining a steady religious life. This charge is generally made by persons who do not appreciate how deeply religion has taken a hold upon the peon. Ceremony, ritual, the supernatural, exert a special influence over him. One cannot travel in Mexico without realizing that the Mexican Indian is in his way deeply religious.

In the United States, certain Protestant denominations have undertaken definite religious work among Mexican immigrants. They claim that the unmet religious needs of the Mexican are many and great, and that they are justified in cultivating a poorly developed field. Catholic leaders, on the other hand,

---

[1] *That Mexican* (New York: Fleming H. Revell Company, 1928), p. 74.

have resented these efforts, feeling that the Protestants are
proselyters. Protestant efforts have met with varied success.
The "converted" Mexican may become an ardent and loyal
Protestant but finds himself somewhat ostracized.

Even after all the best work of both Catholic and Protestant
Christians has been done for Mexican immigrants, the religious
shortcomings of Mexicans, like those of other peoples, are
numerous. There are still large numbers of Mexican immigrants whose religious attitudes are undeveloped and primitive,
meaningful only in personal crises.

Catholic priests who work among Mexican immigrants report that perhaps 90 per cent of the Mexicans are Catholic
and that these may be divided about half and half into "regular
Catholics" and "irregular Catholics." The latter do not attend
church except on special occasions. In a study of Mexicans in
Los Angeles in 1932, S. M. Ortegon analyzed the Mexicans
into Catholics, Evangelicals or Protestants, speculative religious
cults, and free thinkers. Of the Evangelicals, the Methodists,
Baptists, Presbyterians, Pentecostals, Mormons, and Seventh
Day Adventists have made considerable headway. The speculative religious cults include spiritualists, theosophists, and Rus-
sellites. The free thinkers may be divided into communists and
atheists, according to their major centers of interest.[2] Mr.
Ortegon describes the religious traits of the Mexican as being
"a combination of contradictory elements in which we can discover his profound, innate religious sense with a genial but in-
definite faith in God and His goodness to rule the universe.
This produces in the Mexican mind an optimism in his outlook
which, strangely enough, is often tinged with fatalism."[3] Perhaps the fatalism is an outgrowth of the harsh and uncertain
conditions of life, which the Mexican too often has known, im-
pinging upon a people of sensitive feelings.

Catholic priests show a great deal of patience in their contacts with Mexicans. They recognize the handicaps and weaknesses of their humble parishioners. In connection with their
religious duties they often maintain an extensive community

_____

2 For an extensive description of these religious divisions see the
Master's thesis by Samuel M. Ortegon, *The Religious Status of the Mexican
Population of Los Angeles*, University of Southern California, 1932.

3 *Ibid.*, p. 27.

welfare program and render a great deal of informal social service.

The Mexican immigrant with religious training is submissive to authority. He has learned "to follow, to obey, to imitate." Patience and obedience have been ingrained in him by religious training.[4] On the other hand, some of his number are rebelling against this religious influence and are becoming atheistic, radical, and communistic. Their reactions against the church are bitter.

Art is a kind of religion to the Mexican. He has natural tendencies of an artistic nature. Whether seated under a tree, or leaning on a hoe and talking with a compatriot matters little, for in either case he is in himself a picture.

The following contribution comes from an educated Mexican immigrant, who was a student a few years ago in one of the evening classes in the public schools of Los Angeles.[5] In expressing this fine bit of philosophy Mr. Regil discloses something of the richness of what he might contribute to American life were he given a fair opportunity.

People, Clouds, and Sky

I love people.
Each person that I meet
Shares something in common with me.
If we cannot understand the language,
We understand the eyes;
Faces speak a common tongue.
Each one is different,
Yet we are also alike.
We are brothers and sisters of one family,
Humanity.

I love the clouds
That live so at-home in the sky.
On quiet days or glad
They travel their course
Along the pathway of the sky.
O, that we may travel
Our pathway here on earth,
In harmony with life,
Conscious of the beauties of the earth.

---

4 Helen W. Walker, "Mexican Immigrants and American Citizenship," *Sociology and Social Research*, 13:465-71.
5 Taught by Mrs. Nancy J. Bowen.

I love the sea—
The inexorable strength of it,
The laughing lightness of its playful days;
I love its calm, unhurried, inevitable victory
Over all things human.
It is like God.[6]

The Mexican *corridos* are ballads made up of doggerel verse and sung to "a catchy refrain." They reveal the daily life and problems of the people in a folk-music fashion. Dr. Paul S. Taylor prints the "Corrido Pennsylvanio"[7] in which outdoor workers in the cotton fields give their "terrifying" impressions of "the first sights, sound of machinery in a modern steel plant." One glance within and they "come out running at eighty miles an hour." [8]

With education the Mexican produces poetry of no little worth. Not only does it reveal the details of human longings but also the outlines of a philosophy of life.[9]

The Mexican's love of colors is most striking. It is evident in his pottery, his glassware, his toys, his sketches and paintings, his wood carving, his lacquered ware, his basket weaving, his serapes, rebozos, sombreros and other wearing apparel, and also in his care for flowers. The Mexican is both literally and figuratively a colorful person. His interest in art is both simple and far-reaching.

The Mexican is vitally interested in handicraft. He is nimble and artistic with his fingers, not only on the guitar but in making simple works of art. If he comes from northern Mexico he is less skilled in handicraft than if he comes from central or southern Mexico, but yet his bent is unmistakable.

Seldom is there a Mexican home so mean that it does not have its spot of beauty. It may be a tiny flower garden protected by wares and sticks; it may be some colored handwork on the table or on the chair; or, it may be the shrine in the

---

[6] R. Aguilar Regil, Los Angeles, California, *Sociology and Social Research*, 13:435.

[7] *Mexican Labor in the United States: Bethlehem, Pennsylvania* (Berkeley: University of California Publications in Economics, 1931), pp. vii-ix.

[8] *Ibid.*, p. ix.

[9] An interesting study on Mexican *Corridos* is being made at the present time by Nellie M. Foster, Los Angeles, California.

corner where bits of color, bright pictures, and cheap images and trinkets are gathered. The visitor has the feeling that here are people who never forget that hyacinths are as necessary as bread to human life.[10]

One of the differences between Mexicans and many people of the United States is partly shown in the reactions of each to the best music. Materialistic ends often defeat the American's appreciation of music. A Mexican reports:

One time I read of an American family down in Mexico who were playing a very beautiful symphony record on the victrola. They were all talking and laughing, but outside was a Mexican laborer. He stopped, took off his hat, and listened. When he walked on there were tears in his eyes because of the beauty of the piece.

I was riding down in a car with a young American through H— P—. There was a beautiful sunset, the sky was gold-red. It thrilled me as I looked at it. I called the American's attention to the sunset. He was polite enough to look up and remark "beautiful," then in the same breath he went on to talk about machinery. The Americans are too matter-of-fact, materialistic. They lack sentiment and joy that they might gain from the beauty of nature. If they go out for a ride it is to go somewhere and perhaps dance or see a moving-picture.[11]

---

[10] Ruth A. Allen, "Mexican Peon Women in Texas," *Sociology and Social Research*, 16:140.

[11] From interview materials submitted by Charles A. Thomson and obtained by A. E. M.

CHAPTER X

CHILD WELFARE AND THE SECOND GENERATION

When the Mexican peon's child in the United States reaches school age, he may be in no shape at all for his new responsibilities. He may not have had proper food or other needed care. It is not likely that his teeth have had proper attention, or that in case of contagious diseases he has had adequate medical supervision. Without a knowledge of the English language he arrives in school only to be found in competition with children who speak English and who thus have a great advantage.

Moreover, he may have received little help or encouragement from his parents. The one bright hope is the sympathetic "American" teacher. Under her tutelage he makes a creditable showing. During his first years of schooling he does as well as American children in penmanship, about as well in manual work, and three fourths as well in vocabulary, arithmetic, and memorization tests.. For a variety of reasons, some of which have already been indicated, he shows less initiative. His language handicaps, his inferior habits of living, the uncertain labor conditions which affect his parents generally explain his tendency to fall behind, to grow discouraged, and to drop out of school in the early teens. Whether the intelligence tests do him justice or not may be a disputed question, but the results indicate that on the whole he falls below "American" children in intelligence. While some persons believe that the Mexican child reaches his natural learning climax at the beginning of adolescence, it is doubtless true that the environmental handicaps are sufficient to account for many of the failures charged up to him.

Many Mexican children in school are "overaged." In a San Bernardino County study,[1] Dr. M. E. Hill found that 78.5 per cent of the Mexican children were overaged, as against 33.3 per cent of the "American" children. The Mexican children

---

[1] Merton E. Hill, *The Development of an Americanization Program,* Chaffey Junior College, Ontario, California, 1928.

averaged four years behind the "American" children in grade placement.[2]

An interesting study made recently in the San Antonio Public Schools points strongly to the conclusion that prognosis at school entrance "is likely to underestimate the future abilities of the Mexican child." It was found that in a comparison of two groups of Mexican children without school experience the intelligence quotients were similar. In another comparison of two groups where one had school experience and the other had not, the intelligence quotients of the first group were seven points higher than the intelligence quotients of the second group. "The implication is that school experience (or other contemporaneous factors) was responsible for the difference between the older and the younger Mexican siblings."[3]

Uneducated Mexican parents are opposed to education for their children or unappreciative of its merits. When the nut-picking, the cotton-picking, or the beet-cultivating season comes, the children are taken out of school. Illiterate parents do not coöperate in the enforcement of the compulsory education laws, but naturally enough, in view of their own lack of vision and of their economic stress, encourage their children to stay out of school. Without parental coöperation, teachers and attendance officers are seriously handicapped. One teacher who presents the situation at its worst states:

> The schools are opened and the American children are prompt in their attendance. But threats and force from diligent truant officers cannot seem to make an effective impression on the Mexican population of the city. In trucks or wagons, buggies or Fords, entire Mexican families go out into orchards, and camp there until the picking time is over. The women and the children pick up the nuts, while the men shake the trees and load the sacks.[4]

As the parents become educated, they fall in line with compulsory education. They understand the need for educating their children, even though their own education has come late

---

2 *Ibid.*, pp. 54, 77.

3 E. Lee Davenport, "The Intelligence Quotients of Mexican and non-Mexican Siblings," *School and Society*, 36:304-6.

4 Helen W. Walker, "Mexican Immigrants and American Citizenship," *Sociology and Social Research*, 13:59.

or has been cut short. Teachers report splendid coöperation from this type of parent.

Often the social distance between the teachers and the Mexican child is less than that between the parents and the child. For example, a girl secretly wrote and sent a note to her teacher, explaining how her mother was keeping her home needlessly, and that she wanted the teacher to understand. "Don't let my mother know that I am sending you this letter, or she will give me the stick."

Mexican parents usually object to school segregation for their children. Of course there is a great deal of geographic and economic segregation, for Mexicans commonly live in camps or semi-isolated communities. However, Mexican communities sometimes extend into "American" areas and Mexican children may number half or more of the enrollment at a given school.

In the natural segregation schools, located "beyond the tracks," "in the hollow," or "down at the camp," the Mexican parents often feel certain that their children are discriminated against by boards of education, and that their children are the last to be accorded new equipment, buildings, and the like. In the mixed schools, "American" parents often remonstrate against the association of Mexican children with their children, feeling that the health at least of their children is endangered.

The school that is deliberately segregated by the public education authorities is at first objected to by Mexican parents, but is later accepted. The change in attitudes runs a course somewhat as follows: In such a school, all the Mexican children start, to a degree, on an equal basis. At least there is not the discouraging presence of "American" children who speak English fluently. The Mexican children are not so likely to develop feelings of inferiority. They compete against other Mexican children. They make better progress as a rule than when thrown at six years of age into school with "American" children. When they have spent five or six years in a segregated school they are often able to compete fairly well with "American" children. They have acquired a good knowledge of English; many are able then to give a good account of themselves when entering a school where there are "American" children of their own ages. They develop a confidence in themselves that otherwise would not be theirs. On such a showing, even Mexican parents who have been opposed to segregation have come to see its merits and to support it.

The Mexican's attitude toward segregation is like that of the rest of the world. He does not like to be segregated if segregation means a lowered status. If segregation implies a higher status, he seeks it. If it is imposed on him, he is likely to react against it. If he has a voice in its inception, he may favor it. If the children's status in the long run is pushed upward and he has a long-term vision, then he may support the idea of segregation.

The legality of compulsory segregation of Mexican children was questioned in California in 1929, and the Attorney General of the state, U. S. Webb, ruled that he found "no authority in the law of this state for the establishment of separate schools for Mexicans." [5] The Attorney General ruled that schools, with special class hours for Mexicans or other children who work on farms, could be maintained, as long "as all children of the school district are privileged to select the schools which they desire to attend." Such decisions represent the spirit of fair play, but they do not guarantee, of course, that all parents who do not want their children to come in contact with Mexican children will experience a lessening of prejudice.

To meet the educational needs of children whose parents are employed in seasonal industries, the migratory school has been devised. It provides, at least partially, for the needs of these children. Different methods have been developed; one of the earlier schools has been described as follows:

In January, 1926, the Chaffey Union High School, California, established a traveling school for the labor camps of the district. An old bus body was renovated, put on a chassis, and worked over into a school room. Instead of the regular bus seats, folding chairs were used; a movable blackboard, a drop table, cabinets with several types of sanitary, Red Cross, and other equipment, a miniature bed, scales, and utensils of various types were introduced for class purposes. An electric gong was attached to the bus so that classes might be summoned when the school arrived in camp. This new type of Americanization school has become very useful. Within the first two weeks after it began going to the camps, fifty Mexican women and as many part-time Mexican girls were reached with class work; these had not had the

---

[5] September 7, 1929.

advantage of Americanization work before. The little children of the camps came with their mothers, and began calling the bus "Escuelita", or little school, a name which has held. Since the establishment of this traveling school hundreds of adolescent girls and women have been reached in the labor camps. As many as twenty-six Mexicans have been seated at class work within the narrow walls of "Escuelita."[6]

The second-generation Mexicans have only recently begun to reach later adolescence and early maturity. They are attaining years of discretion in an uneasy state of mind. They are no longer satisfied with many of the culture traits of their parents; they have adopted many of the new ways but are not received into "American" society. They are in a dilemma. They do not wish to turn back, but they cannot go ahead. They cannot secure social recognition, attain occupational status, or escape the unjust stigma of being treated as "foreigners." They cannot dodge discouragement. They solve their dilemmas by falling back upon parental culture, and become disorganized and delinquent.

For the calendar year of 1933 (County of Los Angeles) only 58 of the "Mexican boys" who were filed on were born in Mexico, while 330 were born in the United States according to the Probation Office Report. Only 16 of the "Mexican girls" were born in Mexico, while 100 were born in the United States.[7] It would appear that the second-generation Mexican, born in the United States, constitutes a special problem to himself, to his parents, and to the community, and that the people of the United States bear a special responsibility for his welfare.

To be born in the United States but not accepted into "American" life represents a deplorable condition. To be "American-born" but called "a dirty greaser" by "Americans," creates mental conflicts. The need is for discrimination on the part of "Americans," a discrimination that judges Mexicans on the basis of individual worth and possibilities, and not on color of skin or lack of opportunities.

A number of native-born Mexican boys and girls are reaching the junior and senior high school levels and are doing well

---

6 Merton E. Hill, *op. cit.*, p. 13.

7 Annual Report, Los Angeles County, Probation Department, 1933, p. 3.

in several lines, particularly in the arts and crafts. Weaving classes are popular with the girls. The large percentage, however, do not reach the high schools because of early retardation, lack of encouragement from home, prejudice of other pupils, and special difficulty with one or more school subjects, such as mathematics.[8] The economic status of parents is often a strong hindering factor.

Those who have finished high school find great difficulty in securing appropriate employment. By the people of the United States the second-generation Mexican is regarded like the rank and file of Mexican adults, namely, as a laborer. He cannot overcome this social injustice. If his parents are educated, still he is considered a Mexican and not an "American," and thus is prevented from securing adequate opportunities.

That people in the United States entertain adverse attitudes toward American-born Mexicans is a deplorable fact. After meeting with continued opposition, the citizen of Mexican lineage grows disheartened. At first chagrined, he may even become resentful, and naturally so. At best, it is very discouraging to the second-generation Mexican children to discover sooner or later that they are not being treated as citizens of the United States.

Mexican mothers often sense the problems which their children face, but are perplexed. They are made to feel embarrassed but do not know what to do. A woman whose daughter objects to her wearing a scarf on her head explains:

She says that the "Americans" will look at her and laugh at her if they see her on the street with her mother in one of these. This is the very prettiest of all the scarfs that I have ever had. I do not want the "Americans" to laugh at my S. on account of me. I do not like to wear a hat, because I cannot. I have a hat here that we bought at a sale, but it will not stay on my head. The bus goes so fast all the time. But I do not want the "Americans" to laugh at my S. Why do they laugh at her and not at me? She *must* go with me to town. I cannot speak the English and she must be with me. Do you really think that they laugh at her?[9]

Second-generation Mexicans are intermarrying. Their children constitute an increasingly important group of third-genera-

---

[8] According to a teacher in the public schools of Los Angeles County.
[9] From interview materials submitted by H. W. W.

tion Mexican-Americans. While their grandparents speak chiefly Spanish, while their parents speak both Spanish and English, they are refusing to speak Spanish. They are surely more assimilated than were the preceding generations. The culture traits of the people of the United States are their chief characteristics. Despite all the handicaps, the third-generation Mexican-Americans are better assimilated than the second and, of course, than the first generation.

Acculturation anywhere usually begins with superficials. Mexican children are not backward in responding to superficial culture traits. The adolescents and the young men and women lead the way. "The bobby skirt was practically universal among the girls a short time after it was so popular with the American flapper, as was 'sta-comb' with the boys." A Mexican youth with his black hair slicked back can demand attention at any time that he cares to shuffle down the street in his new suit with his twenty-two inch balloon trousers.[10] A few years ago the question of bobbed hair created a furor in many Mexican homes. The mothers were greatly disturbed when the daughters insisted on cutting their hair. One mother said:

> My Lupe says she will bob her beautiful hair if I say "Yes" or if I say "No." What makes her like that? She knows that her father will beat her if she does not mind us. Since we have been in the United States she has always been a good girl, until now when she says that she will do what she wants. She says that we are funny and that we want her to be funny and like the old people, too. Do you think that the girls will laugh at her in the school if she has long hair? The nurse says for us to let her cut her hair, that it will be good for the hair. Lupe says it is her hair and she will cut it if she wants to. She is young and she will not listen to the ones who know more than she does.[11]

Mexican-Americans who are reaching the age of twenty-one are struggling with the problem of citizenship. If they were not forewarned, they would be looking forward with bright hopes to the day when they might enter into the full privileges of citizenship. The forewarning comes in the shape of the ominous attitudes of parents, of older brothers or sisters, and other associates. Some of the parents have either tried out citizenship and found it wanting, or have heard of its short-

---

10 From interview materials submitted by G. A. S.
11 *Loc. cit.*

comings. In either case the Mexican-American reaches the age of twenty-one with misgivings.

Mexican-Americans are growing up in homes distinctly Mexican in spirit and culture. They have been trained in the public schools and in an "American" environment as citizens. They find themselves in a dilemma, suffering a conflict in attitudes. The home is Mexican; the school is "American." Some adolescents are stimulated to play the dual rôles of being good Mexicans at home and good "Americans" at school. While this problem is not peculiar to Mexicans it becomes especially serious in their cases.

The experiences which trouble the Mexican-Americans most are those in which citizens of the United States continually treat them as "Mexicans." They are native-born, and as such are citizens; they have learned English, acquired occupational skills, and understand something of "American" standards; but when they aspire to recognition they are stunned by being labeled "foreigners," or worse still, "dirty greasers." Like "American" youth they run the gamut from the finest types of human character to low-grade individuals. Many "Americans," unfortunately, do not discriminate; they treat all as inferiors and as foreigners.

CHAPTER XI

CITIZENSHIP AND ADULT EDUCATION

The Mexican immigrant possesses a deep-seated loyalty to his native land. It has been well pointed out that the periods of turmoil in Mexico have keyed the Mexican's feeling to a high pitch. A revolution-disturbed republic, "like a sick and tossing parent," receives "the homage of mystic-loving children." Being repeatedly stirred and excited, the Mexican's feelings become expressed in "a turbulent patriotism." His country's fate has hung in the balances so often that patriotism is kept throbbing. Each crisis that Mexico has weathered has added to the patriotic fixations.

When you inquire of a Mexican immigrant why he is patriotic, he will likely shrug his shoulders and tell you that he just feels that way, but that he cannot explain why. Patriotism appears in the form of powerful feelings organized into lasting sentiment. To change the Mexican immigrant's loyalty from his native to his adopted country requires a realignment of organized sentiment. It is a process more difficult and delicate than the citizens of the United States realize.

The Mexican comes to the United States with expectations. He has imagined many things in the United States at their best. He anticipates few of the problems which will arise. Not all the difficulties of adjustment, even of temporary adjustment, are foreseen. But, like immigrants in general, he suffers unexpected hardships and disappointments. The first impacts are often bewildering. Labor conditions are perplexing, cost of living is high, migratory conditions are puzzling, unemployment is common, turnover is rapid, unheard of laws trouble him and sometimes land him in jail.

The Mexican's first experiences do not arouse his desires to become a citizen. In fact, he neither learns nor thinks of becoming a citizen, and his loyalty to his home country increases rather than decreases. He comes expecting to return. Little happens in his first months' experiences in the United States to change his mind.

After he has been in this country for some time, perhaps a few years, the question of becoming a citizen indirectly reaches his attention. If he utters a serious remark about citizenship, it is likely to be met with jeers from his Mexican associates. Any rising interest that he may have is promptly checked.

There is no movement among Mexican immigrants toward citizenship. The naturalization figures are plain. With the naturalization of Mexicans in recent years averaging around a hundred a year out of an eligible Mexican immigrant population of several hundred thousand, the facts are striking. In a specific California Mexican community of 50,000, it is estimated that not over 200 are naturalized. Elsewhere, similar situations obtain. In the year ending June 30, 1932, for example, a total of 136,111 persons were naturalized in the United States, but of these only 248 were Mexicans.

The non-naturalization of Mexicans may be accounted for in a number of ways: (1) The Mexican's loyalty to his native country. This loyalty is composed of deep-seated feelings that cannot be easily overthrown. A prominent Mexican leader raises a question basic to naturalization of anyone anywhere, when he expresses the doubt that an immigrant can ever foreswear a genuine loyalty to the country which has nourished him in childhood, which includes all that is mortal of his beloved but departed parents, which holds for him precious, undying memories. It is claimed that to such a person, naturalization may mean a hypocritical swearing away of loyalty to home country. A dutiful son cannot really swear away his loyalty to the parents who gave him birth and whom he learned to love, but he can add other loyalties to his parental loyalty, namely, loyalty to his wife and children. In this way, it is argued, an immigrant may develop new and even greater loyalties. At any rate, the Mexican immigrant is not strongly stimulated to develop a new loyalty, or to substitute it for a loyalty which is already strong.

The Mexican immigrant is not dissimilar to Englishmen, Canadians, or others who come to the United States with strong national sentiments. None of these peoples relinquishes powerful sentiments easily. The classic description of an Englishman becoming an American citizen,[1] by H. J. Bridges, contains valuable suggestions to the American who cannot understand why the Mexican does not give up his loyalty to Mexico easily. It is doubtful whether many Englishmen who come to the United States as adults really give up their loyalty to all that is fine and good in the symbolism of the Union Jack, even though they have adopted the Stars and Stripes.

(2) Naturalization does not make adequate changes in the status of the Mexican. Citizenship is disappointing to him, for he is still likely to be treated as a Mexican and a foreigner. Citizens of the United States as a rule do not distinguish between naturalized and unnaturalized Mexicans. "They all look alike," is the superficial explanation and inadequate justification. Since the naturalized Mexican is still treated as unnaturalized, he logically asks, "Why become naturalized?"

Citizenship to the Mexican may mean no gain but an actual loss. While still a Mexican citizen, the Mexican can call on a Mexican consul for aid when he experiences difficulty, but when he becomes a citizen of the United States this assistance is lost. It is a loss grievously felt, for there is not likely to be anyone to take the place of the consul. If the Mexican appeals to the courts in the United States he is confused by legal intricacies. The courts are strange and expensive. His language handicap is serious. He cannot easily obtain redress for grievances. Mexicans who have become citizens in the United States, but who have found the experiment unsatisfactory, exert a widespread influence against naturalization. Not only do the weaknesses of naturalization spread and become exaggerated, but Mexicans who contemplate naturalization are openly ridiculed by their fellows.

(3) Undemocratic practices of people of the United States toward Mexicans who are endeavoring to better their living conditions, make citizenship in our country unattractive. A social worker makes this report concerning two Mexicans who desire to climb to a higher culture level by seeking out property in a middle class section of A— and arranging for its purchase, paying down a definite sum. They believed in America as a land of opportunities for their children and aspired to live in a

---

[1] *On Becoming an American* (Boston: Marshall Jones Company, 1919).

neighborhood where health, play and social contacts would be wholesome. The realtor who had charge of the transaction was promptly bombarded by neighbors with letters, personal calls, threats, all protesting against the sale of property in that neighborhood to Mexicans. The pressure became so urgent that the agent felt obliged to call off the deal and to refund the "down payment" to the Mexican purchasers. The latter were dumbfounded. They had been blamed for being clannish and undesirable because of living in a shabby, unsanitary district; when they sought to get out from the Mexican quarters and to live in a better neighborhood, they were denied the opportunity. It was not difficult for them to feel that "Americanism" is hypocrisy. Speaking to them or to their many friends about becoming citizens in our country after such experiences would be considered a mockery. They prefer to live as self-respecting Mexicans than to live among "holier-than-thou" citizens of the United States. The indictment is severe but has enough harsh experiences to support it and to prevent its complete denial. Whenever the Mexican gets started toward citizenship in our country in its social aspects, his initiative is likely to be checked in the initial stage.

Another case may be cited where a Mexican business man who has made considerable cultural progress in the United States decided to leave the Mexican quarters and rented a house in a neighborhood where "Americans" live. He started to move but was threatened by his future neighbors to the point where he decided to give up his plans. What will be the natural response of this man or of his neighbors when citizenship is suggested?

They talk to us about becoming citizens, but if we become citizens we are still Mexicans. They look at our hair, and listen to our speech and call us Mexicans. Even my boy who was born in the United States is a Mexican it seems. He has to go to the Mexican school. There is always a difference in the way he is treated.[2]

To charge the Mexican immigrant with being unappreciative is beside the mark. He is appreciative of his advantages as much as are other immigrants, but his enthusiasm is tempered by being treated as an inferior, even after he has begun to climb

---

[2] From personal interview materials by H. W. W.

the ladder of success. His negligence has often been put this way: Since he lives in the United States, enjoys the benefits of its high wages, good health conditions, and particularly the advantages of the public schools for his numerous children, he should assume his share of governmental responsibilities or get out of the country. The situation, however, is not entirely different from that of thousands of persons from the United States who have lived a number of years in Mexico and profited greatly thereby, but who have never become citizens there or assumed civic responsibilities. Although the Mexican immigrant sends much money via money orders back to Mexico instead of investing it in the United States, the procedure is more than offset by the millions which are acquired by "Americans" in Mexico and shipped back here.

Neither Mexicans in the United States nor Americans in Mexico change their loyalty attitudes with ease. The former come here to get more wages, and to return; the latter go there to get more profits, and to return. Each is sure that his own country is superior. Nothing happens to either to change his underlying attitudes of national patriotism.

There are Mexicans, however, who have found the naturalization experiment a success. Their experiences are fairly uniform. Each states he has at least "a few fine American friends," and that through these choice persons each has found his new citizenship worth while. Personal friendship is the magic wand. This has developed the Mexican's loyalty to the United States to the point where it has superseded Mexican loyalty. The new citizenship attitude comes at the point of making new personal contacts of a substantial and helpful nature among the people of the United States.

When urged to follow an introductory course in English with a course in civics, the Mexican peon is likely to decline. His "head is too hard." It is difficult to make the necessary adjustments. He may be urged to take a class in government, civics, or citizenship, but the appeal is not strong. To the Mexican the practical values are generally not easily discernible.

Adult education for Mexican immigrants has made considerable progress, although the illiterate Mexican laborer has had little stimulus on the whole to become educated. The victim of seasonal and migratory labor, he moves from place to place, loafs between seasons, reads little, talks rarely with educated people in the United States, and lives in a world of unlettered Mexicans like himself. Stimulated by the urge to secure better wages, he may attend evening classes in English. Sometimes the opportunity for social contacts is a drawing card. The married Mexican laborer does not allow his wife, as a rule, to attend evening classes. The women attend school in the daytime. Special classes for mothers have been carried on to good advantage.

Adult Mexican immigrants make slow progress educationally; conditions are heavily against them. Interruptions are many. They learn the rudiments of English, but more important, they become acquainted with kindly, patient, sympathetic Americans, such as their teachers. These teachers give Mexican immigrants a new and wholesome concept of the United States. A teacher reports:

> The Mexicans are most interesting. The women don't want me to say anything to them in Spanish. The men are sometimes insulted if I don't talk to them in English. The men ask a hundred times a week how much money my car cost, and the women ask how much did my new dress cost. The women beg me to teach them how to cook and they especially want to know how to make chocolate cake and lemon pie. These they cannot purchase. You can please a Mexican woman most of all if you smile at her babies. It is so much easier to get along with her during the day, if you will smile at the babies in the morning.[3]

Despite the lack of education of the Mexican peon and his inability to read English, the Foreign Language Information Service[4] reported that in 1929, at the climax of a period of prosperity there were ten dailies, seventy weeklies, and forty-four monthlies published in Spanish in the United States and that there were eleven additional newspapers published in towns "across the Border" which circulated extensively in the United States. Aside from the latter, the Spanish press is found in twelve different states. These publications influence a large percentage of the Mexican population of the United States, and afford excellent avenues for the development of good will. They are the main agencies of informal adult education.

---

3 From interview materials submitted by G. A. S.
4 With headquarters in New York City.

CHAPTER XII

LEGISLATION AND CONTROL

The Mexican, as is quite natural, feels that his country is superior to the United States.[1] The Mexican immigrant may grant that there are certain advantages to be had in the United States but his loyalty to Mexico remains strong. The Mexican feels that the United States has treated his country unjustly, dating back to the Mexican War in 1846-1848. He believes that the United States is powerful and to be feared. He resents the activities of "Americans" who have come into Mexico and, as he says, exploited his people. He reacts against "American penetration." The giant power to the north has been mistrusted, although the recent work of Ambassadors Morrow, Clark, and Daniels has offset the old attitudes considerably. The "gringos" are still mistrusted.

Mexico, in recent years, has been strongly pro-labor. The United States is credited with being strongly pro-capital. International relations involve the bridging of the labor-capital chasm and overcoming the mutual jealousies. Mexico, disturbed by many revolutions, now believes that she is on the road to stable government; a new degree of nationalism is developing. She is jealous of her progress and must needs be treated as a rising power and as a sensitive people.

Mexico is Latin and Indian; the United States is judged to be Anglo-Saxon. The former has a range of culture traits that seems to be contradictory to certain Anglo-Saxon culture traits; but in reality it is complementary. The Latin and Indian temperaments clash with the "American"; the latter bluntly misinterprets the former.

Mexican immigration increased for a number of years to the point where its restriction was urged with increasing force. When the national Quota Law was first put into operation in 1921, the Mexicans were not included. Again in 1924 no quota

---

[1] In the same way that the patriots in any country feel that their own country is superior to other countries.

restrictions were adopted against Mexicans. The present national origins law holds Mexicans to no quota rule. Canadians are likewise exempted.

It is claimed that Mexicans were not included in the Quota because their labor was needed, particularly in the Southwest. Large-scale agriculture, the railroads, and other business interests have urged that Mexican immigrants be kept off the Quota, so that a liberal supply of desirable unskilled labor would continue to be available.

The restriction demand has been fostered by the racialists, particularly, in the East. They contend that the United States possesses superior racial stock in the Nordics and that the standard must not be lowered by the influx of too many persons from "inferior races." All races of course are inferior to the racialists except their own. At any rate, it is claimed that there are entirely too many low-grade Mexicans coming into the country. Better class Mexicans are not immigrating to any great extent; the low level Mexicans are a racial menace and hence restriction is demanded. The racialists may not be large in number but they are articulate; they speak to large audiences, and they have social power.[2]

A second class of restrictionists is composed of trade unionists. They are jealous of "American" labor standards, which they claim are being lowered by the numbers of Mexicans who are willing to work for less than the "American" standard wage under subnormal housing and living conditions. Unskilled Mexicans cannot be organized readily, and thus their presence hinders the growth of unionism, the strong defense mechanism of the "American" standard of living. The American Federation of Labor went on record first in 1927 in favor of putting the Mexicans on the Quota. "Low wages, long hours, low standards of living on the part of Mexicans, means," said a labor leader at the 1927 meeting of the American Federation, "that the Mexicans are wresting the Southwest from Americans." Organized labor believes in establishing an immigration wall, after the

---

[2] It should also be stated that there are many eugenists and careful scholars who have made studies of biological factors and who have produced some evidence to show the dangers of a large infiltration of Mexican blood into the racial stocks of the United States. Professor Samuel J. Holmes of the University of California is one of the ablest leaders in this group.

manner of organized capital in erecting a tariff wall. The latter wishes to keep out cheap goods; the former, cheap labor.

A third class of restrictionists is composed of social and public health workers. Despite the fact that these people are special friends, often personal friends of the Mexicans, they favor restrictive legislation. They do not want more Mexicans to come until those who are here are better able to take care of themselves than at present. They point out that in the larger cities, barring perhaps an exception or two, the Mexicans constitute an undue proportion of the charity cases; that their percentage in many county hospitals is double their population percentages in the given counties; that the number of Mexicans in the jails in the Southwest is entirely out of proportion; that the danger of contagious diseases originating in Mexican centers is still high in spite of the splendid health work being done for the Mexicans. Even the higher class Mexican, it is pointed out, dreads the arrival of Mexican transient laborers and fears that they may bring disease and sickness to Mexicans already here.

Moreover, the unemployment of Mexicans between "seasons" is cited as a menace. There is a drifting to the cities where unemployment runs high for several weeks in the winter time, and where poverty, delinquency, crime, and ill-health are increased. The high turnover is disorganizing. The employers of Mexican labor are charged with bringing in Mexican laborers, paying their transportation expenses, but leaving them idle for periods of time, and allowing them to become a charge upon the public. The Mexican is "cheap" labor to the "American" employer, it is asserted, but dear to the taxpayers. That the taxpayers are called upon to pay several fold what the employers save, is a common contention.

A fourth group of restrictionists are the public school teachers. They constitute in the main the most loyal friends that the Mexicans have in the United States. They understand Mexican immigrants well and are excellent spokesmen for the Mexicans' needs. They favor restriction on the ground that under present conditions "Americans" are not adequately providing for the Mexicans. As special friends of Mexicans they do not want large numbers coming in, when those already here are living far below "American" standards. They point to the many adverse effects of migratory labor and transient living conditions.

Many Mexican leaders in the Southwest comprise a fifth group of people who advocate restriction of Mexican immigration. A regulated number of immigrants each year will enable Mexican leaders to develop protective and self-help organizations among the lower-class immigrants who are now, it is claimed, exploited by both "Americans" and fellow Mexicans. Large influxes of peon laborers prevent the leaders here from developing an *esprit de corps* among the masses. These leaders, however, feel that restriction and regulation should come from Mexico rather than be imposed by the United States, for reasons that will shortly be discussed.

On the other hand several groups oppose restriction. Employers of labor in the Southwest, especially, place their arguments in this wise against restriction. They point out how they depend on unskilled labor. European unskilled labor is decreasingly available because our restrictive legislation has bottled up the sources. Chinese labor has been debarred from entering the country by legislative action demanded by the West.[3] The Japanese laborer, it is claimed, was so efficient that it took two workers to fill the place which he was forced to vacate.[4] A movement was inaugurated in 1928 to debar by national legislation the further advent of Filipino labor, which is not well fitted to perform the heavier forms of unskilled needs. Native "American" youth are refusing to do rural manual labor. They prefer to live in the cities, caught by the glamour of possible white collar jobs, and the larger opportunities to get ahead.[5] Hence, the need for an unrestricted labor supply from Mexico. All other sources are closed. For these reasons the agriculturists have pleaded strongly for Mexican labor.[6]

---

3 In 1882, 1892, 1902 for the Chinese.

4 In 1908, the "Gentleman's Agreement" was arranged by President Theodore Roosevelt with the Japanese Government whereby the latter agreed to allow no more Japanese laborers to migrate to the United States, barring certain exceptions.

5 Professor T. N. Carver has said that there are "Americans" who will fill the labor needs in question, if they are paid enough. The employer replies that the wages that would have to be paid would be prohibitive.

6 One of them in Imperial Valley, California, stated in 1929 that if the Mexicans are put on the Quota, the Valley as an agricultural region will revert

(Continued on next page)

A second group opposes a quota law for Mexicans because it would be an affront to Mexico. To restrict Mexicans without applying the same rule to Canadians and other Latin peoples in Central America and in South America would create ill will in our sister Republic. Even if all of North and South America were put on a quota, Mexico would feel that such restrictions were directed at her; hence, it is claimed that restriction of Mexican immigration must come as a joint or mutual undertaking. The American Federation of Labor postponed action at one time in the hope, which did not materialize, that a joint agreement might be made between the Mexican Federation of Labor and itself. Some Mexican leaders in Mexico City evidently feel that any restrictive law against Mexicans passed in the United States would lower the status of Mexicans in the eyes of the world.

Then, a third group contends that increased surveillance of the Border, insistence on registration of all aliens including Mexicans in the United States, enforcement of the prohibition to admit anyone who is likely to become a public charge, and further deportation of all who are in the country illegally, will be sufficient. Some claim that the Mexican immigration problem will solve itself if it is left alone. They believe that as conditions improve in Mexico, immigration to this country will decrease, and that increased numbers of Mexican immigrants will return to Mexico. They point to the reclamation and repatriation movements now under way in Mexico, to the advanced and social nature of the labor laws now going into effect in Mexico, and assert that the time is not far distant when Mexican labor will no

---

to a desert. The manager of a Colorado Company when asked what he would do without Mexicans replied: "We'd be out of luck. We'd have to close our factories, and the farmers would lose their crops. We are absolutely dependent on the Mexicans." From Phoenix, Arizona, came the statement: "If a sufficient supply of suitable labor, that is, Mexican, cannot be obtained, thousands of acres under government reclamation projects throughout the West will be forced to quit intensified farming and raise crops that can be produced and harvested with a small amount of labor." In 1928, the Board of Directors of the California Fruit Growers' Exchange, representing eleven thousand citrus growers and investments of about three hundred millions of dollars vigorously protested a quota for Mexicans, asserting that the citrus growers of this state are almost entirely dependent upon Mexican labor, that to restrict the labor supply will curtail the crops and cause an advancement of food prices. Moreover, it is claimed that the climatic conditions in certain arid sections of the Southwest are such that only the Mexicans are physically constituted to perform the work required.

longer wish to come to the United States. They declare that Mexico with its resources and small population is a relatively empty country, and that emigration is already a movement of the past.

Another suggestion, originating with employers of labor, is that Mexican laborers be brought in under contract for a definite period, and be shipped back to the Border when the seasonal labor needs are met. This plan also has the support of some social workers who see in it a method to prevent the increase of the adult charity and criminal cases in this country. The plan, however, is open to serious criticism. Shipping labor by carload lots from one country to another is fraught with administrative and dehumanizing difficulties. Laborers under contract in large numbers are likely "to be treated as cattle."

Although such a plan has been put in operation successfully between France and Italy and between Germany and Czechoslovakia, the conditions there are different, and there is little likelihood that the plan would work here.

To bring in Mexicans to do work that "Americans" consider beneath their dignity and then to send them back, is an adverse reflection upon Mexicans that Mexico will not accept. If there is work that is too far beneath the human level for "Americans" to do, then the self-respecting people of Mexico can hardly be expected to allow their fellow-countrymen to be herded together and shipped into our country to do this work.[7]

A fundamental procedure is to make an industrial survey of the Southwest at intervals, under impartial auspices. One purpose would be to find out exactly how many unskilled laborers are needed, month by month, and place by place, throughout the Southwest. Another purpose would be to discover the numbers of unskilled laborers available in the Southwest, month

---

[7]As a substitute for Mexicans, Porto Rican and Negro labor has been suggested. Limited experimentation has been made with Porto Ricans with the resultant feeling that it is not a success. To bring into the Southwest thousands of Porto Rican and Negro laborers would create serious problems of social adjustment. The prospect is not inviting to the agriculturists. New race problems are viewed with gravity. There is no guarantee that Porto Ricans would be treated other than as a low caste; race riots would develop as have already occurred where Filipino immigrants have become somewhat numerous. The Southwest does not view favorably a large Negro immigration. Race friction, prejudice, and rioting would develop, it is believed, even by trained observers.

by month, and place by place. With both the supply and the needs recorded from time to time, the present unknown situation would become known and a reliable and scientific program of meeting whatever needs are discovered could be maintained.

It is already clear that hundreds and perhaps thousands of Mexicans could be better distributed than now, as far as living in proximity to agricultural needs is concerned. There are also possibilities of developing diversified activities in given localities whereby migratory labor conditions could be done away with, whereby steady employment the year around could be provided, and whereby stimulating living and housing conditions could be developed by the Mexicans themselves in the form of self-respecting and permanent communities and ultimately as citizens of the United States. It behooves "American" industry to solve its own labor problems without leaning heavily on the weak, unorganized, and illiterate people of another nation. Industry in the United States has shown vast acumen in solving many technical problems, far greater than in solving its human problems. All that it needs to do is to turn its attention to its human problems, and these may be solved.

Up to 1928, the United States had treated immigration entirely as a domestic affair. It was this attitude which won for the United States the resentment of Japan in 1924, when the Japanese were excluded from our country. But in the early months of 1928, President Coolidge virtually announced the inauguration of a new policy when he asked that the Mexicans be not put on the Quota. Perhaps this announcement will be viewed by some people as an exception and not as a new policy. Even so, the exception is of more than usual significance, for it has the earmarks of a new policy.

In asking that the Mexicans not be placed on the Quota, President Coolidge stated that quota restrictions would create antagonism in Mexico toward the United States. In other words, our immigration legislation is to be tempered by the feelings of the country concerned. Hence, immigration is no longer to be viewed as a purely national affair. The world is not only growing smaller, but it is being seen as a human unit as well as a set of divided nationalisms. The implication is strong that immigration, or the movement of people from one nation to another, is to be viewed as a human problem that is larger than a national problem.

Another vital phase of the Mexican immigration problem is found in a wide strip of Mexican territory which extends east and west along the Border on the south, from the Gulf of Mexico to the Pacific Ocean. All Mexican immigration to the United States either comes through this territory or originates in it. At certain population centers social conditions are entirely discreditable to both Mexico and the United States. It is deeply colored by the actions of those "Americans" who profit from the maintenance of saloons, gambling places, illicit vice, and by the Mexicans who connive with "Americans" in the maintenance of these "joints." Moreover, these centers are patronized by "ritzy Americans" who rush across the Border to patronize them and thereby disgrace their country and its flag irretrievably. There are numerous Mexicans who are ashamed of these conditions, but who are helpless as long as there is so much "American" money freely poured out.

Through these Mexican focal points of "American" recklessness and waste, Mexican immigrants travel; in these places many receive their first and sometimes most lasting impressions of the United States and of some of its noble ideals. "Most immigrants come through these border towns and sometimes get their first impressions of 'Americans' there."[8]

There is need for a joint "American" and Mexican immigration commission to investigate, discuss, understand, and make recommendations concerning immigration and other questions of mutual concern. Where the broad-minded representatives of two countries can work together upon common problems, more progress of benefit to both countries can be expected than when two groups of self-sufficient national representatives meet secretly miles apart and indulge in wild suspicions and jealousies. Joint commission action is a sound starting point for considering migration as an international process, rather than as a compartment phenomenon divided by political boundaries.

----

[8] From Report of Commission on International and Interracial Factors in the Problem of Mexicans in the United States, George W. Hinman, Secretary, Home Missions Council, Philadelphia, 1927, p. 37.

CHAPTER XIII

REPATRIATION AND READJUSTMENT

While there has been an extensive movement back and forth across the Border for many years, the depression in the fall of 1929 inaugurated a homeward trek of Mexican immigrants larger than had ever been known before. Such a movement is nothing new in the history of immigration. During the past century waves of immigration to the United States from Europe came in times of prosperity, and were uniformly followed by waves of emigration. In recent decades, the Italians led the homeward procession so often that they became known as "birds of passage."

The Mexicans who have "gone back" include: (1) those who have voluntarily packed up their belongings and returned by car or train; (2) those who have returned under polite coercion; and (3) those who have been deported.[1] The second group is composed of many Mexicans who have been told by county or other public welfare agencies that if they would depart their transportation expenses to the Border would be paid, but if they did not accept this proposition they would be denied further welfare aid.

In Mexico a *repatriado* is defined as a person who, having left his country to live a number of years in another country, returns to his own country to reside and to assume the duties of citizenship. According to a leading Mexican official, *repatriados* are regarded in Mexico as the Mexicans who have lived in a foreign country and have returned to the Republic "for the purpose of settling down, regardless of whether they came back of their own accord or were deported by foreign authorities."

From the Office of Social Statistics in Mexico City and through the courtesy of Lic. Ramon Beteta, the author secured the figures given in Table IX concerning repatriates. Table IX gives the data for four years, from January 1, 1930, to Decem-

---

1 The materials of this chapter represent a revision of the article by the writer on "Mexican Repatriates," *Sociology and Social Research*, 18:169-76, November-December, 1933.

ber 31, 1933, inclusive. The high month was November, 1931, flanked strongly by October and December of the same year. The total number of repatriates for the four years was 311,712, which means that by the present writing the total number of Mexican *repatriados* since January 1, 1930 is approaching the third of a million mark. This is a large number of persons to be reabsorbed into Mexico in a depression period. Most of these repatriates, approximately 90 per cent, have come from the United States.[2]

TABLE IX

Mexican *Repatriados*

1930	Nos.	1931	Nos.	1932	Nos.	1933	Nos.
January	3762	—	6627	—	9394	—	3216
February	3446	—	6216	—	6501	—	3291
March	3367	—	7719	—	6151	—	3278
April	3817	—	7448	—	6229	—	5058
May	3719	—	7616	—	8594	—	3120
June	5102	—	9959	—	7927	—	3175
July	5662	—	8465	—	8266	—	2042
August	5522	—	8624	—	6291	—	2550
September	6957	—	9398	—	4302	—	1944
October	8610	—	17092	—	5368	—	2552
November	9679	—	21055	—	5686	—	2816
December	9927	—	14742	—	5939	—	3466
Totals	69570	—	124991	—	80647	—	36508

Where do the *repatriados* go in Mexico? They have returned to their native villages and towns, to the large cities, and to the repatriation colonies established by the government. While it is evident that by far the largest percentage have gone back to their native communities and that only a small percentage have gone to the large cities and to the repatriation colonies, the extent of each of these percentages is not clear.[3] Perhaps we may estimate that about 80 per cent have returned to the villages; 15 per cent to the large cities; and 5 per cent to the repatriation and colonization centers.

---

[2] According to Mexican Government figures obtained by James C. Gilbert.

[3] According to interview materials secured from a Mexican official early in 1933 by Marion Flad, University of Southern California, approximately 85 per cent of the repatriates return to the villages and repatriation centers, and 15 per cent to the large cities.

Those who have returned to the villages have been received into their respective family groups freely, according to the Mexican custom. Shelter and food have been shared with the returning relatives even though no work or additional food was immediately available.

Others have struck out for the larger cities and sought work under metropolitan conditions. A *repatriado* who had lived fourteen years in the United States and who during the summer of 1933 was working temporarily as a painter on the National Theater in Mexico City, said to the writer: "I have made a terrible mistake. I should have stayed in the United States. Opportunities here [Mexico City] are fewer than in the United States." Only the most resourceful are able to get readjusted in the large cities within a reasonable length of time.

Still other *repatriados* have gone to the large government repatriation centers (a total of about 5,000 was reported to be in the two largest centers in July, 1933). Preliminary reports indicate that these centers have not yet succeeded. They involve many changes in ways of living that the repatriate can make only with the greatest difficulty. Large-scale collective establishments call for habits and culture patterns different from those of the small-scale camps to which Mexicans have become accustomed in the United States.[4]

Why do some repatriates succeed in Mexico and others fail? Is adjustment purely a matter of luck, or can some principle or rule be discovered? What effect does advancement of the economic and cultural scale in the United States have upon the returned repatriate? Do education and cultural advancement hinder or help adjustment in Mexico?

Although the repatriates are welcomed by their village relatives, yet the more advanced quickly grow restless. Not being able to transform their native villages, they fall back into the old ways, or else they grow disappointed and scornful. If they be small in number, the falling back process occurs without much delay; but if their numbers be large, they form a kind of recalcitrant minority. A conflict ensues with the result

---

4 Manuel Gamio points out a number of factors which explains the failure of the early repatriation enterprises in Mexico (See his *Mexican Immigration to the United States*, pp. 235 ff.).

that the repatriated minority are called "gringos" because of their superior airs and American ways.[5]

For this reason there arises at times a natural antagonism which is often even unconscious between the characters, automatic attitudes, and tendencies of the reactionary majority and the progressive minority of those who are being repatriated, who are charged with being "Yankified" innovators, Masons or pagans, destroyers of the old customs, freakish, intruders, etc.[6]

The conflict continues until the minority succumbs or some of its leaders go to the large cities, only to find themselves strangers there, although some are able, by their wits, to get ahead.

The picture of the returned Mexican immigrant operating a big tractor in his home community is largely buncombe. Here and there he is able in a minor way to bring about changes in the culture traits of his fellow townsmen or villagers. The blue overall is slowly superseding the more picturesque white cotton suit, but more fundamental changes are coming very slowly. Sometimes the blue denim is worn over "the regulation Mexican white shirt and pajama trousers."[7]

In Arandas, Jalisco, Dr. Paul S. Taylor was impressed more "by the relatively small degree of change in the attitudes and ways of living of the returned emigrants than by the material change which experience in the United States sometimes produced in the economic conditions of individuals." [8] The repatriates easily "slip back into the old ways" after the clothes and money they have brought with them are worn out. However, they find it hard to work for small wages after having received larger ones in the United States. The natives are unwilling to admit the superiority of the repatriates.[9]

Do the various members of a returned emigrant's family adjust themselves with similar ease or difficulty in Mexico? Clearly, no. The father seems to have less difficulty than does the mother or the children, and the younger children less than the older ones. The father has been more accustomed to migration and less attached to any one particular spot in the

---

[5] Emma R. Stevenson, "The Emigrant Comes Home," *Survey*, 41:176.

[6] Gamio, *op. cit.*, p. 236.

[7] Osgood Hardy, "Los Repatriados," *Pomona College Magazine*, 21:73.

[8] *A Spanish-Mexican Peasant Community, Arandas in Jalisco, Mexico* (Berkeley: University of California Press, 1933), p. 55.

[9] *Ibid.*, p. 60.

United States. The younger children have not yet become "American" in any sense. The older children, however, have learned English, acquired "American" ways, made "American" friends; many protest against returning to Mexico. They are more "American" than Mexican. Although their hopes and ambitions may have been dimmed in the United States, still this country is home. Despite the depression and the lack of opportunities to work, the culture level here is higher than in the Mexican village to which they return. Their difficulties are twofold: They do not want to leave their friends in the United States, and they do not feel at home on the culture level of the village life in Mexico.

The mother is in a dilemma. She wants to go back with her husband to Mexico but does not want to desert her older children, who beg to remain in the United States. She faces a divided family. She is pulled strongly in two different ways at the same time.

The repatriation movement presumes that extensive agrarian progress has been made in Mexico and that land with water is available. To be sure, there is plenty of land but not with water to a great extent. Developments of importance, however, are taking place; for example, the National Irrigation System, No. 4, located north and west of Monterey, Mexico, where the impounded waters provide irrigation for 75,000 acres and where perhaps in two years water will be provided for 150,000 acres. The National Government owns the land and rents it or will sell it on a 28 year installment plan. According to James C. Gilbert, repatriates who returned to Mexico with tools and some money are doing fairly well raising cotton and corn although they had previously "gone broke" in Texas raising cotton.[10] Pending the development of agrarian opportunities the outlook for the *repatriados* is limited.

Many Mexican immigrants are returning to Mexico under a sense of pressure. They fear that all welfare aid will be withdrawn if they do not accept the offer to help them out of our country. In fact, some of them report that they are told by public officials that if they do not accept the offer to take them to the Border no further welfare aid will be given them, and

---

[10] From a letter by James C. Gilbert.

that their record will be closed with the notation, "Failed to coöperate." Rumor becomes exaggerated as it passes from mouth to mouth. It takes only an insinuation from an official in the United States to create widespread fear among Mexican immigrants.

The plan of shipping Mexican immigrants to the Border instead of giving them welfare aid has an important financial aspect. Figures secured by James C. Gilbert show that the cost of returning 9,000 Mexicans to the Border from Los Angeles was about $155,000, whereas the welfare cost of taking care of the same number for one year was approximately $800,000.[11]

Questions are being raised concerning the justice of our Mexican immigration procedure. In times of prosperity Mexican immigrants have been "invited" by large-scale employing concerns to come to the United States. They have come, furnishing an alleged "cheap labor" supply. In times of depression when they are no longer an economic asset but a liability, they are sent back to their native communities "penniless—a burden on those already poor." It is not surprising, therefore, that thinking Mexican leaders are inquiring about the justice of such a procedure. Are Mexican immigrants to be sent for again when prosperous times return, to be treated as "cheap labor," and then again to be returned penniless to poverty-laden relatives? Are industry and agriculture under any obligations to neighbors whom they bring into our country under promises of work, when the latter are stranded here in a time of depression? If these people, by virtue of seasonal labor situations, of migratory labor conditions, of special urges by high-pressure "American" salesmen to buy on the installment plan, are unable to save, is anything due them by way of protection in the form of insurance? Is the obligation to them met simply by paying their transportation expenses to the Border or home especially when that home is one with which they have lost touch and which may already be overburdened with poverty? These are a few of the questions raised by those who wish to see justice done in the relations between Mexico and the United States.

---

11 From data being gathered for a Master of Arts thesis by James C. Gilbert, of the University of Southern California, who spent several months in Mexico in 1933 and 1934, studying the problem in a first-hand way.

Difficulties for the Mexicans who remain in the United States face them on every hand. Conflicts in customs and traditions are perplexing. Old ways are precious and new ways forbidden, and yet changes must be made. Lack of knowledge increases the difficulty in bridging the culture chasms.

I do not speak English; my people are slow to learn English, because we live in Mexican camps or villages where we do not need to speak English. I read and write Spanish, but now I shall try to learn English after all these years. I have lived in Los Angeles twenty years. My children all speak English. When Ruth, my first daughter, was ten years old she asked me to give up wearing my *rebozo*. I thought I never could do that. It seemed a part of my old life in Mexico, and I thought of how new and strange everything here seemed when I first came wearing my *rebozo*.[12]

Mexican immigrants are often shocked by the strange and apparently loose relationships between the sexes in the United States. Not only do young women meet young men on grounds of freedom but they often act with misleading frankness and freedom toward Mexican young men.

When we first came here the bathing girls were the most shocking thing to the family. My brother took me to W—. How I loved to go to W—! I was not shocked, but mama said, "The day I see you in those bathing suits, I don't know what I will do." Later on, though, we went to the beach and bathed,—it is just the custom you know. Mama thought there was too much liberty in this country, and still believes so.[13]

There is one way in which they think American young women should be more careful: they should know Latins before they become intimate with them, not because they may not themselves be fine, or their men friends among Mexicans be high-minded youths, but because unless they know something of Latin psychology, they should not be too free with the young men who come north to study, and observe; for, the newly arrived Latin has no reason to suppose the American girl draws any barriers at all, when once he notices how free she is. He simply does not know where she puts the limit, and it is not he that is to be condemned, any more than the girl; they simply must know each other.[14]

Interracial conflicts are baffling. In southern California, for example, where large numbers of Mexicans and Japanese are thrown together, misunderstanding easily arises, for the two

---

12 From interview materials submitted by H. W. W.
13 *Loc. cit.*
14 From interview materials submitted by E. H. M.

cultures are different at many points, and the two sets of
temperaments are likewise far apart.

> You know, Japanese and Mexicans generally do not mix at all. They
> are so different in ways and temperament and seem to mistrust or else mis-
> understand one another. But these two Japanese women live near the Mexi-
> can colony in A—. One has a vegetable market and the other is the wife of
> a nurseryman. They were anxious to learn to speak English. I told them
> we had a night school but that it was Mexican. They begged to come too,
> and so we talked it over at night school and the Mexicans decided to invite
> them.
>
> At first the Mexicans thought these ladies were very funny, and enjoyed
> laughing at them a great deal. But I explained to the Mexicans that the Jap-
> anese have a very hard time to learn English because their pronunciation and
> even their alphabet are so very different from ours. And I finally got them
> to be more friendly and polite.
>
> The Mexicans have come to admire these Japanese women very much.
> They are very bright and learn fast. They are devout members of a Prot-
> estant church. On Wednesday nights they are never at night school as they
> go to prayer meeting then. The Mexicans tell me they think these Japanese
> are fine Christians, better than most Americans, and for that reason they seem
> to admire them a great deal.[15]

Mexicans and Filipinos sometimes clash. Competition for
work is the usual cause. The younger Mexicans are more overt
in their antagonism than are the older people. From V—, California, comes the following account:

> The Mexicans are very hostile to the Filipinos, for economic reasons.
> Last fall, the Valencia crop was unusually small in size, and the Fruit As-
> sociation thought it necessary to cut wages. As the Mexicans refused to
> accept the cut, the Filipinos were promised that if they would work then,
> they would have work when the navel crop came on. Most of the Mexicans
> left V— to pick nuts, and when they returned for the navel season, they
> found that the Filipinos had their jobs . . . . . There have been some fights
> between the two groups. On one occasion, Filipinos were attending the
> night school at the Mexican health center, and some Mexican boys outside
> began calling them names. One of the Filipinos jumped through the window
> and started a fight . . . . . Troubles of this kind are mostly between the
> younger Mexicans and the Filipinos. The older ones resent the presence of
> the Filipinos but do nothing about it.[16]

Then, there is the problem created by the fact that persons
of all races condemn members of other races on the ground of

---

15 From interview materials submitted by H. W. W.
16 From interview materials submitted by E. H.

a single unfortunate experience with a member of that race.[17] Quick generalization on limited experience is a serious evil.

One American will do something bad, then some Mexicans think all Americans are like that, and just the same way. One Mexican is drunk, or one Mexican steals, or one Mexican does something else bad and then Americans think all Mexicans are bad. Just the same, some Americans think all Mexicans are dirty. They are not. S. down here is very dirty, but you know too, Mrs. Y. is very clean. All Mexicans are not clean, all Mexicans are not dirty; all Mexicans are not bad, all Mexicans are not good. We have to know people. No? But I like to live in the neighborhood with Mexicans. I want my children to learn good Spanish; I want my children to go to good American schools to learn good English. It is better for them to know both. *Verdad?*[18]

Thus, the problem of making adjustments grows complicated. The people of the United States can help or hinder greatly in the Mexican's reorganization difficulties. Unfortunately he often shows little interest and the result is a serious loss to the Mexican.

In this struggle to make his adjustments, in this process so full of conflict of cultures, he is unfortunately losing much of the fine old grace of his people, and he is imitating much that is crude while he acquires some that is good. He has a wealth to contribute to this country: love of play, buoyancy of spirit, appreciation of the beautiful, if he is only given a chance to do so.[19]

---

[17] E. S. Bogardus, *Immigration and Race Attitudes* (Boston: D. C. Heath and Company, 1928), p. 243.

[18] From interview materials submitted by H. W. W.

[19] Helen W. Walker, "Mexican Immigrants and American Citizenship," *Sociology and Social Research*, 13:471.

CHAPTER XIV

LITERATURE AND RESEARCH

The literature on the Mexican immigrant falls somewhat naturally into three classes. First, there are the studies of the Mexican immigrant's culture traits and backgrounds. Second, a considerable number of local studies of particular Mexican immigrant communities in the United States have been made and reported upon briefly in print. These are supplemented by numerous general studies of the Mexican immigrant's situation in the United States. Third, a variety of suggestions has been made regarding interracial adjustments. Some of these advocate restriction of Mexican immigration as a means of simplifying interracial relations in this country; others deal almost entirely with the establishment of good will relations between Mexico and the United States.[1]

The books, reports, and articles dealing with the culture backgrounds of Mexican immigrants are legion. A selection, therefore, has been made of some of those which are deemed the most important. The range is wide, extending from ethnological studies to popular interpretations. The need for new scientific studies is also evident. New developments are occurring. New light on old problems is needed.

An understanding of the Mexican immigrant rests directly on knowing his culture traits, and on being able to diagnose the culture conflicts of "Americans" and Mexicans. In so far as the United States is a social and economic problem to the Mexican immigrant, or to the extent that the Mexican is viewed as a problem in the United States, culture conflicts are at the bottom of the whole story. These conflicts require skillful handling. The half-baked prescriptions of chauvinists usually aggravate such conflicts. Programs of racial adjustment wait for their successful culmination upon a thorough understanding of the complex and diverse culture traits of Mexicans by

---

[1] In this chapter the materials available to the English-reading world have been carefully considered and as complete as possible a selection of the best books and articles has been made.

"Americans" and of "Americans" by Mexicans. It is not enough for a few social scientists to possess this knowledge; it is equally important that the pertinent data become a part of our common knowledge.

Albig, William, "Opinions Concerning Unskilled Mexican Immigrants," *Sociology and Social Research*, 15:62-72.

Based on studies in Flint, Michigan, showing the opinions of Hungarian, Serbian, Polish, Negro, and white American neighbors of Mexicans to be on the whole unfavorable, due to the low culture level of Mexicans who were contacted.

Allen, Ruth A., "Mexican Peon Women in Texas," *Sociology and Social Research*, 16:131-42.

The social position, industrial outlook, family problems, and adjustment difficulties of Mexican peon women are described.

Alvarado, E. M., "Mexican Immigration to the United States," *National Conference of Social Work*, 1920: 479-80.

Presents a favorable picture of the lower classes who come for economic betterment. Also describes the aristocracy who come for political, educational, and business reasons.

American Federation of Labor, *Proceedings 47th Annual Convention*, Washington, D.C., pp. 95, 321, 336.

Report of the American-Mexican Labor Immigration and Emigration Conference, with memorandum of agreement between the American Federation of Labor and the Mexican Federation of Labor.

Applegate, Frank, "Spanish Colonial Arts," *Survey*, 66:156-57.

Gives insight into the Spanish-New Mexican arts.

Arnold, Charles A., *The Folklore, Manners and Customs of the Mexicans in San Antonio, Texas*. Master's thesis, University of Texas, Austin, 1928.

Atl, Dr., "Popular Arts of Mexico," *Survey*, 3:161-64.

Special attention is given to pottery and weaving.

Austin, Mary, "Mexicans and New Mexico," *Survey*, 66:141-44, 187-90.

A treatment of the Mexican in New Mexico from 1598 to the present time. The Mexican finds expression not "in the possession of things" but "in songs and dancing, in the making of pottery, and manners."

Babcock, Cora C., "Housekeeping in Mexico," *Overland*, 43:207-10.

In describing her experiences with Mexican help in her own home the author states that they are careless and uneducated, but honest, good-natured, and take reproofs kindly.

Baca, Emilie M., "Panchita," *The Family*, 8:44.

A brief narrative of the unregulated childhood of a Mexican girl, revealing primitiveness of emotional life.

Baldwin, J. M., "Notes on Education in Mexico," *Nation*, 82:132.

Advocates that the United States should send official delegates to Mexico to hold conventions and study their systems and vice versa.

Bamford, Edwin F., "Mexican Casual Labor Problem in the Southwest," *Journal of Applied Sociology*, 8:363-71.

Discusses the following questions: (1) Why do Mexicans come to the United States? (2) Into what occupations do they enter and in which of these are they most efficient? (3) What American conditions tend to promote industrial instability among Mexican immigrant workers? (4) What traits do these immigrants possess which, if properly developed, would tend to solve the Mexican casual problem? (5) Are Mexican immigrants economic and social assets or liabilities?

————, "Industrialization and the Mexican Casual," *Proceedings of Southwestern Political and Social Science Association*, Austin, Texas, March, 1924.

A discussion of the Mexican laborer in Texas, giving a number of detailed observations.

Batten, James H., "The Mexican Immigration Problem," *Pan-Pacific Progress*, 8:39, 52.

Restriction is favored, but the quota plan is opposed, for it would be disastrous to agriculture.

————, "Mexico's Program: An Opportunity," *World Tomorrow*, 12:36-39.

Favors restrictions but not unfair ones that would arouse Mexican antagonism.

————, "Our Cultural Relations with Mexico," *Proceedings of the Institute of International Relations*, 7:47-52, 1930, University of Southern California, Los Angeles.

Scholarships for exchange students with Mexico are urged.

Beals, Carleton, *Mexico: An Interpretation*. New York: B. W. Huebsch, Inc., 1923.

The third part of the volume on "The Social Fabric" is an interpretation, partly sociological, of the life of Mexicans.

————, "Mexican as He Is," *North American Review*, 214:538-46.

A description of the character, hospitality, economic and living conditions of the Mexican in Mexico.

Bell, P. L., *Mexican West Coast and Lower California*. Government Printing Office, Washington, D.C., 1923.

In this survey by the Department of Commerce, data are given concerning educational, industrial, and living conditions in the regions indicated.

Birkinbine, J., "Our Neighbor Mexico," *National Geographic Magazine*, 22: 475.

Describes geographical and topographical phases of Mexico as well as the various classes of people.

Blakeslee, George H., *Mexico and the Caribbean*. New York: G. E. Stechert and Company, 1920.

A large portion of the volume is devoted to such themes as: "Mexican People," "Indian Contribution to Mexico," "Factor of Health in Mexican Character," and "Reconstruction Problems in Mexico." The book reproduces a series of lectures given at Clark University in 1920 at the Conference on International Relations.

Bloch, Louis, "Report on the Mexican Labor Situation in Imperial Valley, 1926," *22nd Biennial Report, Bureau of Labor Statistics,* Sacramento, California, 1925-26.
  Indicates an extensive dependence on Mexican labor.
Boas, Franz, "Notes on Mexican Folk-Lore," *Journal of American Folk-Lore,* 25:204-60.
  A scientific discussion throwing light on many of the Indian backgrounds of Mexican immigrants.
Bogardus, Emory S., "Mexican Repatriates," *Sociology and Social Research,* 18:169-76.
  Describes the repatriation movement and its resultant problems.
————, "The Mexican Immigrant," *Journal of Applied Sociology,* 11:470-88.
  Four types of Mexican immigrant communities are described; the basic occupations together with wages and hours are discussed. The culture patterns and problems of these people are analyzed; personality and social disorganization problems are treated. Assimilation difficulties are noted.
————, "Second Generation Mexicans," *Sociology and Social Research,* 13: 276-83.
  Native born, but still treated as foreigners, "greasers," Mexicans. Neither they nor their parents receive much encouragement to enter into the social life of the United States. Blocked at nearly every turn they grow skeptical.
————, "The Mexican Immigrant and the Quota," *Sociology and Social Research,* 12:371-78.
  Presents arguments for and against putting the Mexicans on the Quota.
————, "The Mexican Immigrant and Segregation," *American Journal of Sociology,* 36:74-80.
  Because the Mexican immigrant has few opportunities to come into contact with "Americans," he does not develop loyalty to the United States or become a citizen. School segregation is a special problem.
————, *Essentials of Americanization,* Ch. XVI, "The Mexican Immigrant." Los Angeles: Jesse Ray Miller, 3rd edition, 1923.
  A summary of Mexican immigrant traits, together with a statement of Mexican immigrant problems in the United States.
Borah, W. R., "Neighbors and Friends, A Plea for Justice to Mexico," *Nation,* 124:392-94.
  "God made us neighbors—let justice make us friends. The first step toward justice is to stop making false and unfair statements about Mexico."
Bowyer, H., "Social Welfare Work in Rural Mexico," *Bulletin of Pan-American Union,* Washington, D.C., 56:453-58.
  Tells of the efforts being made to encourage sanitation, better housing, home hygiene, child care, education, recreation.
Bringas, Esperanze, "The Educational Missionary," *Survey,* 52:172 91.
  New missionaries of education that are sent out by the Mexican government are changing the modes of living.

Bryan, Samuel, "Mexican Immigrants in the United States," *Survey,* 28: 726-30.

Although the Mexicans have proved to be efficient laborers in certain industries, they possess counterbalancing traits, such as low standards of living, lax morals, and slight political interest.

Burgess, T., "On the American Side of the Rio Grande," *Missionary Review,* 50:689-92.

Interracial contacts and needs are discussed.

Burnett, J. L. R., "The Mexican Dancing Girl," *Outing,* 23:378.

A descriptive poem beginning, "A sudden tumult of wild melody."

Butter, Mrs. J. W., "Women of Mexico," *Missionary Review,* 39: 181-86.

Home life and labor conditions are described and illustrated.

Callcott, F., "The Mexican Peon in Texas," *Survey,* 44:437-38.

The study divides the Mexican peons in Texas into two classes: those who intend to make the state their home, and those who come only for the cotton picking season and return as soon as it is over.

Callcott, Wilfred H., *Liberalism in Mexico, 1857-1929.* Stanford University: Stanford University Press, 1931.

Describes social conditions in Mexico prior to 1910 and the aims of the leaders since that date.

Calles, Plutarco E., "A Hundred Years of Revolution," *Survey,* 52: 133-34.

A brief statement of a long struggle for social justice.

Camblon, Ruth, "Mexicans in Chicago," *The Family,* 7:207-11.

During the fiscal year of 1925, 214 per cent of the total foreign-born "under care" families of the United Charities of Chicago were Mexican; 61 per cent of these lived in the Hull House area.

"Caravan of Sorrow," *Living Age,* 332:870-72.

Mexicans migrating to the United States are a loss to Mexico for they rank above the others in character, industry, and intelligence, but to keep them in Mexico, social and economic conditions need to be improved.

Carillo, Alfonso R., "Mexico Looks at the United States," *Sociology and Social Research,* 15:558-61.

Thirteen sets of opinions of Mexicans concerning the United States are given.

Carr, Harry, *Old Mother Mexico.* Boston: Houghton Mifflin Company, 1931.

A journalist vividly reports his observations in travelling about in Mexico.

Case, Alden B., *Thirty Years with the Mexicans: in Peace and Revolution.* New York: Fleming H. Revell Company.

Mexicans are depicted through the eyes of a devoted Protestant missionary.

Chase, Amanda M., "Santa Susana," *Survey,* 66:161-62, 190-93.

A very human story of some of the domestic problems of a Mexican husband and wife in the United States.

Chase, Stuart, *Mexico, A Study of Two Americas.* New York: The Macmillan Company, 1931, 338 pp.
Covers village life, food, drink, housing, labor, play, politics, and other phases of Mexican conditions.
————, "Mexicans Know How to Play," *Harper's Magazine,* 162:672-79.
"The fiesta is the outstanding exhibit of Mexican recreation."
Children's Bureau, *Child Labor and the Work of Mothers in the Beet Fields of Colorado and Michigan.* Bureau Publications No. 115, Washington, D. C., 1923.
Relates in part to the Mexican, who comprises 7 per cent of the workers studied; child labor, education, family income, and health are considered.
Cleland, Robert G., *The Mexican Year Book,* 1922, 1924. Los Angeles: Times-Mirror Press, 1924.
Gives statistical and documentary data concerning agriculture, commerce, education, emigration and industrial conditions in Mexico. A handbook by a member of the faculty of Occidental College.
"Committee of Business Men to Aid Mexico," *Survey,* 34:347-48.
An account of how the American Red Cross formed a committee of financiers and others to help noncombatant Mexicans.
Commissioner-General of Immigration, "Annual Reports," 1918 to 1934. Government Printing Office, Washington, D. C.
Gives statistical data and official comments.
Congressional Hearings, "Should Quota Law be Applied to Mexico?" *Congressional Digest,* Vol. 7, No. 5, May, 1928.
Arguments pro and con are presented by a number of interested persons.
————, "Seasonal Agricultural Laborers from Mexico," before the committee on Immigration and Naturalization, House of Representatives. On H. R. 6741, 7559, 9036, January 28, 1929; February 3, 9, 11, 23, 1926. Washington, D. C.: Government Printing Office, 1926.
————, "Immigration from Countries of the Western Hemisphere," *Ibid.* On H. R., 6455, 10955, 11687, February 21 to April 5, 1928. Washington, D. C.: Government Printing Office, 1928.
————, "Restriction of Western Hemisphere Immigration," before the Committee on Immigration, United States Senate. On S. 1296, 1437, 3019, February 1, 27-29, March 1, 5, 1928. Washington, D. C.: Government Printing Office, 1928.
Conley, E. M., "Americanization of Mexico," *American Review of Reviews,* 32:724-25.
The influences of American capital and of the interchange of teachers between Mexico and the United States are described.
Connell, Earl M., *The Mexican Population of Austin, Texas.* Master's thesis, University of Texas, Austin, 1925.
Cormack, Joseph M., and Frederick F. Barker, "The Mexican Labor Law," *Southern California Law Review,* VII:251-94.
The analysis appears under twenty-eight headings; eighteen probable future developments in Mexican labor laws are suggested.

Corpio, M. del, "Americans and Mexico," *Survey*, 36:642-43.
Claims that we should send to Mexico our men of science, educators, sociologists who can make themselves admired and respected.

"Cost of Living in Mexico," *Monthly Labor Review*, 13:558-68, 1921.
Gives index figures from 1918 to 1921, showing high peak in August, 1920.

Crawford, R., "Menace of Mexican Immigration," *Current History*, 31:902-7.
Considers certain ways in which Mexicans exert a negative influence in American life, especially by their low standards of living and ill-health.

Creel, George, *The People Next Door*. New York: John Day and Company, 1926.
Has been summed up as "an interpretative history of Mexico and Mexicans" by a journalist, who was motivated by a desire to help the United States see Mexico through understanding eyes.

Culp, Alice B., *A Case Study of Thirty-Five Mexican Families with Special Reference to Mexican Children*. Master's thesis, University of Southern California, Los Angeles, 1927.
Deals with housing, food and clothing, and health conditions, child welfare, moral and religious life, education, and recreation.

"Cultural and Social Coöperation with Mexico," *Bulletin of Pan-American Union*, Washington, D. C., 62:176-78, 1928.
The program for coöperation by Pomona College, California, is described.

Cushing, W. W., "The Distribution of Population in Mexico," *Geographical Review*, 11:227-42.
Gives geographic origins of Mexican immigration to the United States.

Davenport, E. L., "Intelligence Quotients of Mexican and Non-Mexican Siblings," *School and Society*, 36:304-6.
Prognosis at the entrance of the Mexican child in school is likely to underestimate his future ability.

Deering, T., "Music as a Welder of Races in California," *Playground*, 17:234.
Oxnard, California, endeavored to find out what the Mexicans wanted and then help them get it. The first thing wanted was "rebote," a Mexican national game; the second was a Latin-American Community Organization.

Delmet, Don T., "A Study of the Mental and Scholastic Abilities of Mexican Children in the Elementary School," *Journal of Juvenile Research*, 14:267-80.
Finds Mexican children retarded and urges a program including visiting teachers.

De Negri, Ramon P., "The Agrarian Problem," *Survey*, 52:149-52.
Large-scale landholding has been the curse of Mexico.

Dewey, John, "From a Mexican Note-book," *New Republic*, 48:239-41.
Discusses Mexico as a land of contradictions, the cheapness of life in Mexico, the imitation of things both good and evil.

Dickerson, R. E., "Some Suggestive Problems in the Americanization of Mexicans," *Pedagogical Seminary*, 26:288-97.

A survey of Mexican boys of teen-age of Tucson, Arizona, who are under the direction of the Y.M.C.A. of that city.

Dobie, J. Frank, "Ranch Mexicans," *Survey*, 66:167-70.

The ranch Mexican or *vaquero* is a very real factor on the broad expanses of certain sections of Texas, and his life has interesting features.

Drake, Rollen H., *A Comparative Study of the Mentality and Achievement of Mexican and White Children*. Master's thesis, School of Education, University of Southern California, Los Angeles, 1927.

The study is centered in Tucson, Arizona, and includes 144 Mexican children and 173 white children. The former are found to have lower mentality than the latter.

Esquivel, S. I., "The Immigrant from Mexico," *Outlook*, 125:131

Whole villages are migrating to the United States but they need more than wages, namely, better housing, educational facilities, and recreational advantages.

"Exchanging Educational Facilities with Mexico," *Literary Digest*, 68:26-27.

Business interests are furthering exchange scholarships.

Fairchild, H. P., *Immigrant Backgrounds*. New York: John Wiley and Sons, 1927. Chapter XI.

The traits of life and character of Mexicans are depicted.

Farrell, G. A., "Homemaking with the Other Half Along our International Border," *Journal of Home Economics*, 21:413-18.

Points out the peculiar nature of the Mexican's own culture and its influence upon the "American" children in the border counties of Arizona who live in the midst of this culture.

Fellows, Lloyd W., *Economic Aspects of the Mexican Rural Population in California with Special Emphasis on the Need for Mexican Labor in Agriculture*. Master's thesis, University of Southern California, Los Angeles, 1929.

Analysis of farm acreage in California and the extent to which Mexican labor is used.

Fergussons, Erna, "New Mexico's Mexicans," *Century*, 116:437-44.

New Mexico is described as a bilingual state with a wide array of interesting interactions.

Fisher, Irving, "What Mexico Thinks of Us," *Survey*, 36:386.

Mexicans do not distinguish between the attitudes of our capitalists and the honest wishes of the American people as a whole.

Frank, Eva A., "The Mexicans Simply Won't Work," *Nation*, 125:155-57.

Presents contrasting attitudes toward work of Mexicans and "Americans," with reasons for the differences in standpoint.

Freytag, J., "Some Mexican Manners and Customs," *Travel*, 27:32.

Experiences with and descriptions of some of the customs of the Mexicans are given.

Fuller, Elizabeth, "The Mexican Housing Problem in Los Angeles," *Studies in Sociology*, Monograph 17, University of Southern California, 1920.
Describes the Mexican's lack of responsibility and urges better housing.

Galarza, Ernest, "Life in the United States for Mexican People," *National Conference of Social Work*, 1929: 399-404.
Considers the needs and interests of Mexican immigrants in the United States along three lines: economic conditions, educational development, and social status.

Gamio, Manuel, *The Mexican Immigrant, His Life-Story*. Chicago: University of Chicago Press, 1931. xiii and 288 pp.
A wide variety of life-history stories forms the basis of this study which throws new light on the nature of Mexican immigrants.

————, *Mexican Immigration to the United States*. Chicago: University of Chicago Press, 1930. 262 pp.
Discusses from the Mexican viewpoint the reasons for the immigration of Mexicans and the problems of adjustment. Contains a complete report of the author's extensive study of money orders sent back to Mexico by Mexican immigrants. Chapters are given on interracial relations, culture backgrounds, mentality of Mexican immigrants, songs of the immigrant, immigrant attitudes and institutions, social mobility.

————, "The New Conquest," *Survey*, 52:143-46, 192-94.
Describes the new program of social realignment between the races in Mexico.

————, *Preliminary Survey of the Antecedents and Conditions of the Mexican Immigrant Population in the United States and the Formation of a Program for a Definite and Scientific Study of the Problem*. Social Science Research Council, New York, 1928. 146 pp.
Special attention is given to immigration and emigration figures, and to special factors such as money sent back to Mexico by immigrants.

————, "Quantitative Estimate, Sources and Distribution of Mexican Immigration into the United States," Mexico City, 1930. 19 pp.
A summary supplemented by twenty-nine tables and maps.

————, "The Sequence of Cultures in Mexico," *American Anthropologist*, 26:307-22.
Extends from the Archaic to the Pueblo culture.

Garretson, O. K., "A Study of Causes of Retardation among Mexican Children in a Small Public School System in Arizona," *Journal of Educational Psychology*, 19:31-40.
The main cause of retardation is probably in a lack of mental ability.

Garth, Thomas R., "The Intelligence of Mexican School Children," *School and Society*, 27:791-94.
In all, 1,004 Mexican school children of Texas, New Mexico, and Colorado were tested, and were found to have a lower mentality than American children and to be retarded greatly.

————, "A Comparison of the Intelligence of Mexican and Mixed and Full-Blood Indian Children," *Psychological Review*, 30:388-401.
It is concluded that probably differences in opportunity and in mental attitude account in part for differences in intelligence scores and in school attainments.

————, "The Industrial Psychology of the Immigrant Mexican," *Industrial Psychology*, 1:183-87. Different persons compare Mexican workers with workers of other races. The unselfishness, cheerfulness, and kindness of the Mexican worker are emphasized.

Goday, Mercedes, *When I Was a Girl in Mexico*. Boston: Lothrop, Lee and Shepard Company, 1919.
Deals particularly with child life in Mexico. A volume of sketches.

Godkin, E. L., "Mexicanization," *Nation*, 23:365-66.
Curiously insists that the South is Mexicanized, whereby the forms of law and the machinery of justice are treated as weapons of war.

Goldberg, Benjamin, "Tuberculosis in Racial Types with Special Reference to Mexicans," *American Journal of Public Health*, 19:274-86.
Mexican death-rate from tuberculosis in Chicago is ten times that of the general population.

Gonzales, Kathleen M., *The Mexican Family in San Antonio, Texas*. Master's thesis, University of Texas, Austin, 1928.

Goodrich, J. K., *The Coming Mexico*. Chicago: A. C. McClurg and Company, 1913.
A presentation of Mexican life, history, municipal development, and mountaineering in the Diaz period.

Gruening, Ernest, *Mexico and Its Heritage*. New York: The Century Company, 1928.
The author has (1) indicated the agrarian basis of Mexican history, (2) shown the background of the so-called religious conflict, (3) clarified the economic basis of Mexican militarism and politics, (4) discussed the issues underlying the differences between the United States and Mexico, and (5) given interesting chapters on justice, education, health, women, and cultural trends.

Gwin, J. B., "Social Problems of Our Mexican Population," *National Conference of Social Work*, 1926:327-32.
A lecture discussing Mexican immigration, labor, and living conditions.

————, "Back and Forth to Mexico," *Survey*, 39:9-10.
A brief statement of the effects of the World War and of the new literacy test upon Mexican immigrants.

————, "Immigration Along Our Southwest Border," *Annals of the American Academy of Political and Social Science*, 93:126-30.
Explains why and how Mexicans cross the border, and urges a more effective control.

————, "Making Friends of Invaders: Mexican Refugees in Advance of the Returning Troops," *Survey*, 37:621-23.
A study of the Mexican migration to Columbus, New Mexico, when 2,800 refugees arrived ahead of General Pershing's troops.

Hackett, C. W., "Success of Lindbergh's Good Will Mission to Mexico," *Current History*, 27:727-29.
A brief descriptive review is given of reactions of Mexicans.

Hagar, George J., *Plain Facts About Mexico*. New York: Harper and Brothers, 1916.
A brief summary of facts is submitted concerning Mexico's natural, racial, and economic features for the benefit of the American business man.

Hale, Susan, *The Story of Mexico*. New York: E. P. Putnam and Sons, 1889.
Written in story form, and taken from a diary of an extensive traveler in Mexico, describing personal contacts and glimpses.

Hallomon, James A., "Mexico's People Classified and Analyzed," *Literary Digest*, 64:68-75.
A newspaper reporter describes in the Atlanta *Constitution* a number of the social and economic contrasts that he observed in Mexico.

Hamby, William H., "In Search of Senoritas," *Sunset*, 52:24-26.
There are four classes of women in Mexico; the degree of liberty which each woman possesses depends upon the class to which she belongs.

Handman, Max S., "The Mexican Immigrant in Texas," *Southwestern Political and Social Science Quarterly*, 7:33-41.
Three groups of Mexican population in Texas are described: (1) political refugees, wealthy, educated, sophisticated; (2) Texanos, or descendants of the original Texas Mexicans; and (3) casual laborers of recent and transient migration.

————, "Economic Reasons for the Coming of the Mexican Immigrant," *American Journal of Sociology*, 35:601-11.
The Mexican comes to do hand labor in cotton, to work in truck gardens, to fill the needs caused by Negro migration into the North, to meet needs caused by the shutdown of European immigration, to supplant tenant farmers in Texas.

————, "Nationality and Delinquency: The Mexicans in Texas," *National Conference of Social Work*, 1930: 133-45.
"The delinquencies of the Mexican are tied up largely with the nomadic life which he is leading and with the dislocation and disorganization which takes place within a person when he is torn from his village community with its system of control and plunged into a new and strange and, in the main, disorganized environment."

————, "San Antonio, The Old Capital City of Mexican Life and Influence," *Survey*, 66:163-66.
There are 90,000 Mexicans out of a total population of 285,000; they are alert, sensitive, intelligent, and ambitious.

Hanna, P., "Culture and the Intellectuals," *Nation*, 112:585-87.
Describes the attempt under José Vasconcelos to abolish illiteracy in Mexico and to make Mexico the center of culture in the Spanish-speaking world.

Hanson, Stella E., *Mexican Laborers in the Southwest*. Master's thesis, Pomona College, Claremont, California, 1926.

Hapgood, Norman, "Public Opinion on Mexico," *Annals of the American Academy of Political and Social Science*, 132:176-79.
Believes that the United States should frankly state its apparent position of wishing to help its private capitalists in developing Mexico.

Harby, L. C., "Texan Types and Contrasts," *Harpers Magazine*, 81:229-46.
Describes different types of Mexicans found in Texas; tells how they live, how they try to make a living, and describes some of their customs and ceremonies.

Hardy, Osgood, "Los Repatriados," *Pomona College Magazine*, 21:71-73.
Based on personal interviews in Mexico.

Harris, James K., *A Sociological Study of a Mexican School in San Antonio, Texas*. Master's thesis, University of Texas, Austin, 1927.

Hayen, C., "Studying Mexican Relations at El Paso." *Missionary Review*, 50:110-12.
Summarizes a Protestant conference on religious work among Mexicans.

Heald, J. H., "Mexicans in the Southwest," *Missionary Review*, 42:860-65, 1919.
The author, superintendent of Congregational Missions in New Mexico, Arizona, and West Texas, finds two problems: the Spanish-American, and the Mexican proper, and discusses the differences.

Henton, J. M., "Honesty and Courtship in Mexico," *Outlook*, 89:950-60.
The author recites some of his experiences during a residence of three years in Mexico.

Herring, Hubert C., and Katharine Terrill, *The Genius of Mexico*. Committee on Cultural Relations with Latin America, New York, 1930.
A set of lectures containing materials covering the vital phases of Mexican life and character.

Hill, Merton E., *The Development of an Americanization Program*. Chaffey Junior College, Ontario, California, 1928.
A dissertation written for the University of California for the Ed.D. degree. Surveys the school statistics of San Bernardino County relative to Mexican children and their problems. Gives outlines and educational program.

Hinman, George W., Secretary, *Report of Commission on International and Interracial Factors in the Problem of Mexicans in the United States*. Home Missions Council, Philadelphia, 1927.
Contains sections on "Mental Attitude of Mexican Immigrants," "Influence of Mexican Immigrants in the United States," "Prejudice Toward Mexican Immigrants."

Holmes, Samuel J., "An Argument Against Mexican Immigration," Commonwealth Club (San Francisco), II, No. 12:21-27.
Argues from the biological point of view against Mexican immigration.

———, "Perils of Mexican Invasion," *North American Review*, 227:615-23.
Draws up items in a general indictment of Mexican immigration into the United States: (1) a drain upon our charities; (2) disproportionate amount of delinquency; (3) health menace; (4) labor problems; (5) special school needs because of low mentality; (6) reaction in diminishing white population; (7) loyalty to Mexico.

Hoover, Glenn E., "Our Mexican Immigrants," *Foreign Affairs*, 8:99-107.
Takes up the confusion in American public opinion regarding Mexicans and attributes it in part to the confusion of races in Mexico. He favors restriction of Mexican migration from across the southern Border.

Hughes, Lois S., *A Comparative Study of the Intelligence of Mexican and Non-Mexican Children*. Master's thesis, University of Texas, Austin, 1928.

Hunt, R. D., and Nellie V. Sanchez, *A Short History of California*. New York: Thomas Y. Crowell Company, 1929.
Part III deals with Southwestern United States when it was under the rule of Mexico. Seven chapters present the main historical data of this period from a social and economic viewpoint.

Hymer, Evangeline, *A Study of the Social Attitudes of Adult Mexican Immigrants in Los Angeles and Vicinity*. Master's thesis, University of Southern California, Los Angeles, 1923.
Treats of the material arts, myths, family life, and attitudes toward religion, property, and government.

Janvier, T. A., "Mexican Superstitions and Folk-lore," *Scribners Magazine*, 5:349-59.
Affords an insight into the nature and rôle of myths and superstitions among primitive Mexicans in Mexico several decades ago.

Johnson, Alvin S., "Mexico in San Antonio," *New Republic*, 7:190-91.
Finds the Mexicans of San Antonio to be, on the whole, a worthy people.

Johnson, W. T., "Bell Towers and Capitals," *Survey*, 66:158-59.
A picture of the Spanish-New Mexican architecture.

Jones, Anita E., "Mexican Colonies in Chicago," *Social Service Review*, 2: 579-97.
The Mexican population of Chicago, estimated in 1928 at about 10,000, live in well-defined urban colonies or in suburban railroad camps. Special attention is given to schools, recreation, employment, housing, and cultural backgrounds.

Jones, Chester L., *Mexico and Its Reconstruction*. New York: D. Appleton and Company, 1921.
An interpretation of Mexico by a diplomat with insight into Hispanic nature; includes materials on racial traits and social and economic organization.

Jones, Robert C., and Louis R. Wilson, "The Mexican in Chicago," Chicago Church Federation, 1931. 32 pages (pamphlet).
Gives a picture of "20,000 Mexicans" in Chicago as seen through Protestant eyes.

Jurup, H. A., "Some Adventures of an Amateur Propagandist," *Christian Century*, 43:1420-22.
> Relates interesting but adverse experiences in telling American audiences "the good things" about Mexico.

Kalet, Anna, "Mexican Child Welfare," *Survey*, 46:49-50.
> A report of a Child Welfare Congress in Mexico, January, 1921.

King, E. S., "My Mexican Neighbors," *Survey*, 37:624-26.
> Characterization of Mexicans in San Diego. Their loyalty is based on feelings of personal response rather than on any generally accepted "American" standard of living.

Kirk, William, "Cultural Conflict in Mexican Life," *Sociology and Social Research*, 15:352-64.
> City ways are gaining at the expense of folkways in Mexico but sharp culture conflicts are common.

————, "Current Social Movements in Mexico," *Sociology and Social Research*, 15:403-16.
> Three social movements are depicted: the agrarian revolution, rural education, and the new nationalism.

Kirkbride, W. H., "An Argument for Mexican Immigration," Commonwealth Club (San Francisco), II, No. 12:11-20.
> Views of an engineer for the Southern Pacific Railroad.

Knox, W. J., *The Economic Status of the Mexican Immigrant in San Antonio, Texas.* Master's thesis, University of Texas, Austin, 1927.

Landazuri, Elena, "Why We are Different," *Survey*, 52:159-60.
> Indian peoples in Mexico are characterized by lack of organization.

Laut, A. C., "Why Mexico Needs our Help," *Forum*, 64:404-9.
> Discusses ways in which big-hearted United States may assist Mexicans.

Lawrence, D. H., "New Mexico," *Survey*, 66:153-55.
> A novelist experiences religion and democracy among the native peoples of New Mexico.

Lescohier, Don S., "The Vital Problem in Mexican Immigration," *National Conference of Social Work*, 1927:547-54.
> Urges the education, assimilation, and guidance of the Mexican in the United States; and the checking of Mexican immigration temporarily.

"Little Mexico in Northern Cities," *World's Work*, 48:466.
> Some of the best farms of northern states have imported Mexican labor, giving them work for about four months. Not used to having money, many Mexicans spend it foolishly and then rely on charity support.

Lofstedt, Christine, "The Mexican Population of Pasadena, California," *Journal of Applied Sociology*, 7:260-68.
> A concrete study of 1,736 Mexicans in regard to housing, renting, earning a livelihood, insurance, religion, education, mutual understanding.

Loftin, J. O., *Mexican Secondary Education as Developed in the Sidney Lanier Junior High School of San Antonio, Texas.* Master's thesis, Educational Department, State Teachers College, Greeley, Colorado, 1927.

Lyle, E. P., Jr., "American Influence in Mexico," *World's Work*, 6:38-43.
A study of some of the ways in which Mexico responded to American influence prior to 1903.

Mackey, Druzilla R., "Books Without Print," *Survey*, 68:400-1.
Three of these "books" of Mexican peons are: the phonograph, the flower garden, and color.

Manuel, H. T., *The Education of Mexican and Spanish-Speaking Children in Texas*. University of Texas, Austin, 1930. 173 pp.
Herein are many statistics with conclusions concerning the Mexican school child and youth of Texas.

Marston, H. D., "Mexican Traits," *Survey*, 44:562-64.
A study of and experiences with Mexicans while at the Neighborhood Settlement House, San Diego, California. Mexican traits are cited as sense of humor, a sense of decorum, courtesy, and gratitude.

Martin, Percy F., *Mexico of the Twentieth Century*, (2 volumes). New York: Dodd, Mead and Company, 1907.
The first volume describes the industrial development, population, religion, education, home life, sports. The second deals with the different states of Mexico, giving some of the special characteristics of each.

Marvin, George, "Monkey Wrenches in Mexican Machinery," *Independent*, 120:350-53.
Putting Mexico on the Quota without consulting her is disastrous to good will.

Matthews, Amanda, "Some Mexican Girls," *Overland*, 41:163-69.
A characterization of the different types and classes of Mexican girls with illustrations.

McCombs, V. M., *From Over the Border*, Council of Women for Home Missions, New York, 1925.
Gives a sympathetic and understanding consideration of Mexican immigrants from the Protestant religious standpoint.

————, "Rescuing Mexican Children in the Southwest," *Missionary Review*, 46:529-32.
Shows how an American does not know what it means to be born a Mexican baby in a peon family, and how such a child needs to be freed from the bondage of superstition.

McCormick, E. O., "Mexico Welcomes San Francisco Envoys," *Overland Monthly*, 81:28-30.
Tells what occurs on excursion of business men to Mexico.

McDowell, John, *A Study of Social and Economic Factors Relating to Spanish-Speaking People in the United States*. Home Missions Council, Philadelphia, 1927.
Gives an extensive summary.

McEuen, William, *A Survey of the Mexicans in Los Angeles*. Master's thesis, University of Southern California, Los Angeles, 1914.
Useful for comparative purposes with more recent studies; it presents numerous local statistics.

McKenney, R. S., "Mexican Amusements," *Overland*, 46:397-401.
    Describes the "Burning of Judas" and a bull fight. The latter is called
    a science.
McLean, Robert N., *That Mexican*. New York: Fleming H. Revell and Com-
    pany, 1928.
    The first half of the book is devoted to the Mexican in his own country,
    particularly in relation to his economic, social and religious problems;
    the second half considers the main problems which the Mexican faces in
    the United States.
————, "What do you Know About the Mexicans?" *Missionary Review*,
    53:183-87.
    Summarizes types of employment and living conditions.
————, "Getting God Counted Among the Mexicans," *Missionary Review*,
    46:359-63.
    Describes the work of a "community house" under Protestant aus-
    pices.
————, "Rubbing Shoulders on the Border," *Survey*, 52:184-85.
    "We touch the Mexican at only a single point of contact, the industrial,
    and it is just there that hatreds have beginning." Explains why Mexi-
    cans do not become citizens.
————, "Mexican Workers in the United States," *National Conference
    of Social Work*. 1929: 531-38.
    Distinguishes between primary and secondary users of Mexican
    labor in the United States.
————, "Goodbye, Vincente," *Survey Graphic*, 46:182-83
    First-hand observations on repatriation when the movement began.
————, "The Mexican Return," *Nation*, 135:165-66
    Analysis of initial problems of returning Mexicans.
————, "Dyke Against Mexicans," *New Republic*, 59:334-37.
    Considers the movement of Mexican Labor from agriculture to industry
    as the basis for immigration restriction agitation.
McLean, R. N., and Charles A. Thomson, "Spanish and Mexican in Colorado,"
    Board of National Missions of the Presbyterian Church in the U. S. A.,
    New York, 1924.
    Presents detailed information on agricultural conditions.
McWilliams, Carey, "Getting Rid of the Mexicans," *American Mercury*,
    28:322-24.
    "The amiable Mexican never objected to exploitation when he was
    welcome, and now he acquiesces in repatriation."
"Mexican-American Friendship," *Pan-American Magazine*, 29:221-29.
    A Mexico City daily has inaugurated a page of views and editorials
    printed in English, addressed to Americans and Englishmen.
"Mexican Invaders of El Paso," *Survey*, 36:380-82.
    States some of El Paso's problems in caring for revolutionary refugees.
"Mexican Invaders Relieving our Farm-Labor Shortage," *Literary Digest*, 66:
    53-54.
    Mexicans have put Texas on the map agriculturally, and helped to
    put southern California's fruits and vegetables on the national market.

"Mexican Journeys to Bethlehem," *Literary Digest*, 77:103-4.

Explains the contract of the Bethlehem Steel Company with the Mexican consul at San Antonio, Texas, for several thousand Mexicans to work in the steel mills.

"Mexican Labor Colony at Bethlehem, Pennsylvania," *Monthly Labor Review*, 33:822-26.

A study in industrial and racial facts of a colony that has become self-sustaining.

"Mexican Miners Going Back Home," *Survey*, 39:97-98.

A brief statement of the difficulties of Mexican miners with the Arizona Copper Company, including a copy of the telegram sent to President Wilson by the miners.

"Mexican Rights in the United States," *Nation*, 115:51-53.

Accounts of humiliation and hardships suffered by Mexican immigrants are described.

"Mexican Students in American Colleges," *School and Society*, 5:166-67.

Urges scholarships and aid to Mexican students.

Mexicans in California. Report of Governor C. C. Young's Mexican Fact-Finding Committee, San Francisco, 1930, 214 pp.

The statistics are brought up to June 30, 1928, and relate to occupations, wages, labor unions, health, relief, delinquency, crime, naturalization.

"Mexicans in Los Angeles," *Survey*, 44:715-16.

Presents an illiteracy table made from a study of 1,081 Mexican families in Los Angeles; a study of housing conditions, and a statement of delinquency problems.

Mexico, Lectures before the Inter-America Institute, Claremont, California, 1919.

Gives extensive materials on social, economic, and political life in Mexico.

"Mexico-United States Immigration Conference," *American Federationist*, 32:921-25.

Speeches in behalf of labor by President Green and Senor Morones are presented.

Murray, Katharine K., "Mexican Community Service," *Sociology and Social Research*, 17:545-50.

The essence of this type of social service is coöperation between the public school and the Mexican home. Four types of contacts are explained.

Noll, Arthur H., "Musical Mexico," *Lippincott's Monthly Magazine*, 60:424-28.

"The waltz gives place to the polka, the mazurka, and the schottische, and all give way to the jarabe and the danza."

Nordhoff, C. B., "The Human Side of Mexico," *Atlantic Monthly*, 124:502-9.

Describes social life and customs of Mexicans in both California and Mexico.

Norton, Henry K., "Mexican Impressions," *Annals of the American Academy of Political and Social Science*, 138:74-78.

Mexico's problem is to telescope the centuries and to use decades instead of centuries for the social evolutionary process.

Ortegon, Samuel, *The Religious Status of the Mexican Population of Los Angeles*. Master's thesis, School of Religion, University of Southern California, Los Angeles, 1932.

Gives the religious history of Mexicans in Los Angeles since 1781 and surveys the present religious divisions of Mexicans: Catholics, Evangelicals, Cults, and free-thinkers.

Otero, Adelina, "My People," *Survey*, 66:149-51.

An understanding interpretive statement of the Spanish-Americans of New Mexico by one of them acting in the capacity of a school teacher.

Oxnam, G. Bromley, "Mexicans in Los Angeles from the Standpoint of the Religious Forces of the City," *Annals of the American Academy of Political and Social Science*, 93:130-33.

The social conditions of three groups of Mexicans: (1) descendants of early settlers; (2) refugees; and (3) laborers, are described.

Panunzio, Constantine, *How Mexicans Earn and Live, A Study of the Incomes and Expenditures of One Hundred Mexican Families in San Diego, California*. Berkeley: University of California Publications in Economics, 1933.

Covers the fields of income and expenditures, makes comparisons with other cost of living studies, and includes six individual family budgets.

Parr, Eunice P., *A Comparative Study of Mexican and American Children in the Schools of San Antonio, Texas*. Master's thesis, School of Education, University of Chicago, 1926.

Relative progress in certain school subjects in the first grade and home environment, and in other conditioning factors are described.

Paschal, F. C., and L. R. Sullivan, *Racial Differences in the Mental and Physical Development of Mexican Children*. Comparative Psychology Monographs, III, No. 14, 1926.

Paul, G. F., "Mexican Hacienda; Its Place and Its People," *New England Magazine*, 30:198.

Phillips, Hubert, "The School Follows the Child," *Survey*, 66:493-95, 524-25.

An account of the work of migratory schools for Mexican children in California.

"Play for the Mexican Population in Topeka, Kansas," *Playground*, 13:26-27.

A park with apparatus and manned by paid workers was dedicated in 1914 in Topeka to the Mexican settlement. Special benefits have resulted.

Porter, Katherine A., "Corridos," *Survey*, 52:157-59.

"A race of singing people. . . . used to sorrowful beginnings and tragic endings."

Provost, F., "New Life in Mexico," *Pan-American Magazine*, 25:33-39.

Citations from Señor Cabrera's speech before the American Academy of Political and Social Science are reproduced.

Raley, Helen, "Guardians of our Border," *Sunset*, 57:30-31, 62.

Tells of the "bootlegging" of immigrants over the Mexican border.

"Reaching Mexicans in the United States," *Missionary Review*, 50:50-51.

Outlines a procedure along Protestant lines.

Redfield, Robert, *Tepoztlan, A Mexican Village*. Chicago: University of Chicago Press, 1930. xi-247 pp.

A piece of social description in which the author takes the village of Tepoztlan, a community of about 4,000, located fifty miles from Mexico City, and gives a cultural account of a people, chiefly Indian, who are passing from a folk song to a popular song stage and whose close-up contacts with an urban world are disorganizing. Chapters appear on magic, holidays, literature, and village organization.

————, "The Calpolli-Barrio in a Present-Day Mexican Pueblo," *American Anthropologist*, 30:282-94.

The "Calpolli" is "a group of kin" and a "barrio" is a politico-hereditary unit. Tepotzlan furnished the setting for this study.

Regil, R. Aguilar, "People, Clouds, and Sky." *Sociology and Social Research*, 13:435.

Rembao, Alberto, "What Should be Done for Juan Garcia?" *Pomona College Magazine*, 17:145-48.

A program is suggested by a Mexican leader.

Remington, Frederic, "An Outpost of Civilization," *Harpers Magazine*, 88:71-81.

Life on the hacienda San Jose de Bavicara is described and illustrated.

"Renaissance of Mexican Culture," *American Federationist*, 33:279-80.

Tells how the Mexicans who have been forced to accept the culture of another race are trying to find again the customs and culture of their fathers.

"Results of Admission of Mexican Laborers, under Departmental Orders, for Employment in Agricultural Pursuits," *Monthly Labor Review*, 11:1095-97.

Finds no detrimental economic situation resulting from influx of Mexican labor and that Mexicans are not appreciably displacing other white labor.

Review, The Mexican, Washington, D. C., 1916-1920.

This journal was devoted to the enlightenment of the American people concerning the constitutionalist government of Mexico.

Ritchee, R. W., "Making Friends for America," *Sunset*, 49:22-23.

Kind deeds of an American mining engineer in Mexico are reviewed.

Roberts, K. L., "The Docile Mexican," *Saturday Evening Post*, 200:39-41, 165-66.

Supports the view that the United States does not need large numbers of Mexicans and that the Quota is advisable.

————, "Wet and Other Mexicans," *Saturday Evening Post*, 200:10-11, 137-42, 146.

Presents data concerning Mexican immigrants who have crossed the Border illegally.

————, "Mexicans or Ruin," *Saturday Evening Post*, 200:14-15, 142-54.
> The fancied welfare of the pocketbook must not be put ahead of national welfare.

Saenz, Moises, "Mexico, an Appraisal and a Forecast," Committee on Cultural Relations with Latin America, New York, 1929.
> Interpretative address given before Seminar conducted by H. C. Herring.

Saenz, M., and H. I. Priestly, *Some Mexican Problems.* Chicago: University of Chicago Press, 1926.
> The book contains chapters on "Integrating Mexico through Education," "Humanism and the Mexican Laborer," and "The United States and Mexico."

Santiago, Hazel D., "Mexican Influence in Southern California, "*Sociology and Social Research*, 16:68-74.
> The various Mexican ways that are evident in Southern California are sympathetically indicated.

Sauter, Mary, *Arbol Verde: Cultural Conflict and Accomodation in a California Mexican Community.* Master's thesis, Claremont Colleges, Claremont, California, 1933.
> Discusses the second generation and related problems.

"The Seminar in Mexico," Committee on Cultural Relations with Latin America, New York, 1929.
> A stenographic report, giving the substance of lectures by Moises Saenz, Diego Rivera, Rafael Ramirez, and others, on Mexican Life.

"The Seminar on Relations with Mexico," Boston, 1928.
> A stenographic account of a series of lectures by Moises Saenz, E. A. Ross, R. Trevino, and others on conditions in Mexico.

Sheldon, W. H., "The Intelligence of Mexican Children," *School and Society*, 19:139-42.
> Gives the results of a comparison of 100 white and 100 Mexican children according to the Stanford Binet Test, with the latter falling .15 below the former.

Shontz, Orfa J., "The Land of 'Poco Tiempo,' " *The Family*, 8:74-79.
> Studies in Mexican family relationships in a changing social environment. The Mexican tries to adjust himself to American ways; the result is disintegration.

Showalter, W. J., "Mexico and Mexicans," *National Geographic Magazine*, 25:471-93.
> Describes the resources and the civilization.

Simpich, Fredrick, "Along our Side of the Mexican Border," *National Geographic Magazine*, 38:61-80.
> Describes the adventuresome border country as to geography, population, social life and problems. A splendid ecological study.

————, "The Little Brown Brother Treks North," *Independent*, 116:237-39.
> If Mexican immigrants and others are restricted, Americans shall need to do more manual labor or produce less. No mention is made of new inventions in machinery.

Slayden, J. L., "Some Observations on Mexican Immigration," *Annals of the American Academy of Political and Social Science*, 93:121-26.
Observations made in Texas from three angles: economical, racial, and political.

Spaulding, Charles B., "The Mexican Strike at El Monte, California," *Sociology and Social Research*, XVIII:571-80.
Describes a strike of Mexicans employed by Japanese farmers.

Spence, Lewis, *Mexico of the Mexicans*. New York: Charles Scribner's Sons, 1918.
Urges sympathy for Mexicans, and describes the Mexican character, family life, society high and low, literature, art, music, religion, sports, ranching.

Stanley, Grace C., "Special Schools for Mexicans," *Survey*, 44:714-15.
In San Bernardino, the program which was inaugurated to fit the special needs of Mexicans, was centered on activities and occupations rather than on book study.

Starr, Frederick, *In Indian Mexico*. Chicago: Forbes and Company, 1908.
Gives a first-hand picture of the culture traits of one part of Indian Mexico after another, until the reader begins to feel at home among all the peoples who are described.

Starr-Hunt, Jack, "The Mexican Who Went Home," *Los Angeles Times Sunday Magazine*, March 26, 1933, pp. 10, 20.
A boost for repatriation.

Stevenson, Emma R., "The Emigrant Comes Home," *Survey*, 46:175-77.
Problems of readjustment are presented.

Stine, J. H., "Texas Playgrounds Influence Mexicans," *Playground*, 10:259-62.
Several schools in the Mexican sections have been used for playgrounds with good results. Active play apparently has been unknown to Mexican girls. Mexicans have much potential athletic ability.

Stowell, J. S., *The Near-Side of the Mexican Question*. New York: George H. Doran Company, 1921.
A brief statement of the rôle that Mexicans are playing in the national life of the United States. The chapter on "The Mexican at Work in the United States" gives data and suggestions.

Story, Russell M., editor, *Mexico: Lectures before the Inter-America Institute*. Inter-America Institute, Pomona College, Claremont, California, 1929.
Gives a survey by Mexican and American authorities of social, political, financial and international conditions affecting Mexico.

Stowell, J. S., "The Danger of Unrestricted Mexican Immigration," *Current History*, 28:763-68.
Urges a genuinely bilingual border. Reports that some American-born Mexicans are asking how they may become Mexican citizens.

Strout, R. L., "A Fence for the Rio-Grande," *Independent*, 120:518-20.
Argues against Mexican immigration on national and racial protection grounds.

"Student Diplomats of the Americas," *Survey*, 37, 307-8.
Forty-seven colleges and universities offer scholarships to Mexican students.

Sturges, Vera L., "The Progress of Adjustment in Mexican and United States Life," *National Conference of Social Work*. Chicago: University of Chicago Press, 1920: 481-86.
Considers the Mexican and his background as a basis for his adequate adjustment in the United States.

Sullenger, T. Earl, "Mexican Population of Omaha," *Journal of Applied Sociology*, 88:289-93.
Explains how the Mexicans live in Omaha and what the city tries to do for them.

Tannenbaum, Frank, *Peace by Revolution*. New York: Columbia University Press, 1933.
Full of background materials on race, religion, politics, land reform, labor, and education. Explains the culture traits, the conflicts, the longings, the programs of present-day Mexicans. The repudiation of Spanish influence and a renaissance of the Indian culture heritage is made clear.

————, "Mexico—A Promise," *Survey*, 52:129-32.
"We need to stand humbly before a people come to life."

Taylor, Merl C., *Retardation of Mexican Children in the Albuquerque Schools*. Master's thesis, Stanford University, California, 1927.

Taylor, Paul S., *A Spanish-Mexican Peasant Community, Arandas in Jalisco, Mexico*. Berkeley: University of California Press, 1933.
Gives many facts about a community of Spanish stock in the heart of Mexico. Not the least significant part of the monograph are the plates illustrating types and activities.

————, *Mexican Labor in the United States: Bethlehem, Pennsylvania*. Berkeley: University of California Publications in Economics, 1931, 24 pp.
Explains the origins and the labor and social problems of the Mexicans in Bethlehem who numbered 1,000 in 1923 but who declined to 350 or 400 in 1929.

————, *Mexican Labor in the United States: Dimmit County, Winter Garden District, South Texas*. Berkeley: University of California Publications in Economics, 1930.

————, *Mexican Labor in the United States: Imperial Valley*. Berkeley: University of California Publications in Economics, 1928.
Based on first-hand studies, including popular reactions indicated in the newspapers. The author discusses the Mexican population in Imperial Valley, economic aspects of the situation there, the labor market and labor relations, agricultural and non-agricultural labor, property ownership, Mexican clerks, and business men, education, domiciliary and social isolation.

——, *Mexican Labor in the United States: Migration Statistics.*
Berkeley: University of California Publications in Economics, 1929.
After considering the available statistics, the author concludes that the
number of Mexicans in the United States on June 30, 1928 was
882,680 (a conservative estimate).

——, *Mexican Labor in the United States: Migration Statistics, II.*
Berkeley: University of California Publications in Economics, 1933.
Presents data concerning "Migration of Mexicans into California across
the Southeastern Boundary."

——, *Mexican Labor in the United States: Migration Statistics, III.*
Berkeley: University of California Publications in Economics, 1933.
Deals with the migration of Mexicans into the "Valley of California."

——, *Mexican Labor in the United States: Racial School Statistics.*
Berkeley: University of California Publications in Economics, 1929.

——, *Mexican Labor in the United States: Valley of the South Platte,
Colorado.* Berkeley: University of California Publications in Economics, 1929.
Facts are brought together concerning the economic aspects of the
sugar beet culture, the movement of seasonal labor, housing of beet
laborers, Mexican societies, leasing and owning of property, social
isolation, and Spanish Americans versus Mexicans.

——, "Mexicans North of the Rio Grande," *Survey,* 66: 135-40, 197-205.
A survey of the situation in the United States.

——, "Some Aspects of Mexican Immigration," *Journal of Political
Economy,* 38:609-15.
Summarizes the penetration of Mexican labor into transportation, steel
manufacturing, and meat-packing, indicating how "Americans" have
been displaced.

Thomson, Charles A., "Coöperation in Work Among Spanish-Americans,"
Missionary Review, 41:973-75.
Maintains that all religious agencies, outstanding educators, and social
leaders should coöperate in solving the Mexican's problems.

——, "Linking the Two Americas," *Missionary Review,* 51:619-23.
Good will is the needed link.

——, "Mexicans — An Interpretation," *National Conference of Social
Work,* 1928:499-503.
The Mexican needs to be seen as a person, not as a problem. He is
equipped with a full share of human frailties, but also with a capacity
to grow and develop.

——, "Restriction of Mexican Immigration," *Journal of Applied Sociology,*
11:574-78.
Restriction is advocated, provided the coöperation of Mexico is secured.

——, "The Man from Next Door," *Century,* 3:275-82.
Pleads for national fair play in dealing with the Mexican immigrant
problem.

Thompson, Edythe T., "A Statistical Study of Sickness Among Mexicans in the Los Angeles Hospital," *California State Board of Health*, 1925.
Statistical studies show the excessive degree of sickness among Mexicans. The health hazards caused by the presence in the United States of low-grade immigrant laborers are great.

————, "Public Health Among the Mexicans," Pomona College, Claremont, California, 1928.
Gives data concerning tuberculosis, venereal diseases, and trachoma.

————, "Survey of Mexican Cases where Tuberculosis is a Problem," *California State Board of Health*, 1926.
The economic cost of meeting the Mexican's health needs is high. Suggests the extension of the visiting nurse service, extension of clinical service, and of visiting medical and dietitian services.

Thompson, Wallace, *The Mexican Mind: A Study of National Psychology.* Boston: Little, Brown, and Company, 1922.
An analysis of the Mexican's mode of thinking, his habits of thought and of action, and of his racial characteristics.

————, *The People of Mexico, Who They Are and How They Live.* New York: Harper and Brothers, 1921.
In this "anatomy of Mexico," the author discusses the physical and mental characteristics of the Mexicans, social origins, Mexican population, religion, housing, family life, sanitation, conditions of labor, education, vice, and crime.

Trowbridge, E. D., *Mexico Today and Tomorrow.* New York: The Macmillian Company, 1919.
Presents Mexican viewpoints on a wide range of conditions in Mexico, and contributes to a better understanding of that country.

"Unhappy Mexico — Our Duty," *Outlook*, 133:527-30.
Outlines the duty of the United States to the Mexicans who are being crushed under ignorance, poverty, war, pestilence, and famine.

Urena, Pedro H., "The Revolution in Intellectual Life," *Survey*, 52:165-66.
The new belief is that all Mexico must become educated.

Vasconcelos, José, "Educational Aspirations," *Survey*, 52:167-69.
Public education is now thought in Mexico to be the state's most important function.

Vasconcelos, José, and Manuel Gamio, *Aspects of Mexican Civilization.* Chicago: University of Chicago Press, 1926.
The first author explains the Latin-American basis of Mexican civilization; the second author, the Indian basis of that civilization.

Vincent, Melvin J., "The Proposed Mexican Labor Code," *Sociology and Social Research*, 14:233-37.
Explains a stage in the development of the Mexican labor movement.

Walker, Helen W., *The Conflict of Cultures in First Generation Mexicans in Santa Ana, California.* Master's thesis, University of Southern California, Los Angeles, 1928.
Analyzes cultural conflicts and the accommodation process.

————, "Mexican Immigrants and American Citizenship," *Sociology and Social Research,* 13:465-71.
Americans hinder Mexicans from becoming citizens. The Mexicans find themselves worse off as citizens than as aliens.

————, "Mexican Immigrants as Laborers," *Sociology and Social Research,* 13:55-62.
Various attitudes, both favorable and unfavorable, toward the Mexican as a laborer are presented. Employer attitudes and Mexican peon attitudes are different—a vicious circle develops.

Wallace, W., "Mexico, Before and After the Revolution," *Missionary Review,* 50:186-93.
Discusses four major objectives of Mexicans: (1) to effect self-control; (2) to solve their social and economic problems; (3) to free themselves from foreign control; (4) to check the influence of the church in politics. Suggests ways whereby Americans may help.

Ward, S. R., "The Mexican in California," Commonwealth Club (San Francisco) II, No. 12.
Statements pro and con are given.

"What the People Read in Mexico," *American Review of Reviews,* 31: 687-88.
Lists and describes briefly the leading periodicals that are read widely in Mexico.

Winter, Nevin, *Mexico and Her People of Today.* Boston: Page and Company, 1907.
The customs and other characteristics of the Mexican people are portrayed.

Winton, George B., *Mexico Today.* Missionary Education Movement of the United States and Canada, New York, 1913.
Argues against the "racial defect" theory concerning Mexicans, and for the formulation of sound educational policies.

————, *Mexico Past and Present,* Nashville, Tennessee: Cokesbury Press, 1928.
An account that is both a history and an interpretation, written to help Mexico's neighbors understand her. Concludes with a brief chapter on the Calles administration.

————, "Progress in Mexico," *Methodist Quarterly Review,* 73: 424-36.
A sympathetic review of social changes is presented.

Young, Kimball, *Mental Differences in Certain Immigrant Groups.* Eugene: University of Oregon Publications, I, No. 11, 1922.
A study of nearly 1,000 twelve-year old children in the vicinity of San Jose, California, including many of Latin-American parentage in which the Latin group falls below "Americans."

INDEX

Japan, 88
Japanese, 41, 85, 96
Justice and immigration, 95
Juvenile probation, 55
"Juvenile Research Bulletin," 63

Killick, V. W., 54

Labor, 37, 87
Labor contract system, 40
Labor distribution, 49, 87, 88
Labor turnover, 50
Labor union, 41
Language handicap, 68, 80
Latin temperament, 82
Legislation, 82
Literature, 99ff.
Living conditions, 27
Los Angeles, 18, 34, 48, 53, 65, 72
Lottery-mindedness, 61
Lumber camp, the, 42

Manana, 46, 47, 52
Mariahuana, 55, 73
Marriage, 29
Materialism, 67
McLean, R. N., 34, 61, 63
Mestizos, 16
Metropolitan Mexicans, 18
Mexican-Americans, 74, 75
Mexican Federation of Labor, 42, 86
Mexican War, the, 82
Mexico, 11, 13, 17, 18, 28, 36, 42, 47, 87, 88, 91, 93
Migratory school, 71
Migratory family, the, 30
Migratory laborer, the, 34
Model camps, 22
Molokans, Russian, 58
Money orders, 48
Morals, 61ff.
Mothers, Mexican, 25, 26, 28, 73
Musical ability, 60

Naturalization, 77, 78
Negro labor, 87
New York City, 81
Nordics, 83
Nurses, Mexican, 44

Organization, community, 22
Organized labor, 41
Ortegon, S. M., 64
Oxnam, G. Bromley, 11
Ownership of homes, 31

Panunzio, C., 32, 35, 39
Park and Burgess, 18
Parental education, 56
Paternalism, 48, 52
Patriotism, 76
Pauperism, 49
Peon, the, 23, 24, 36, 42, 46, 49, 51, 52, 68, 85
Personal reorganization, 49, 98
Philanthropy, 48
Police records, 53
Population in the United States, Mexican, 16
Porto Rican labor, 87
Poverty, 46ff.
Prejudice, 27
Priest, Catholic, 64
Probation officer, 56, 57
Professional people, 38
Property, 33, 46ff.
Protestantism, 63

Quota laws, 82, 83, 88
Quotient, intelligence, 56, 68

Racialists, 83
Railroad labor, 37
Ranch labor, 37
Readjustment, 90ff.
Realtors, 79
"Rebozo," 66, 96
Regil, R. Aguilar, 66
Religion, 17, 25
Repatriation, 90ff.
Research, 99ff.
Restrictionists, 83ff., 88
Roosevelt, Theodore, 85

San Antonio, 69
San Bernardino County, 68
Sanchez, Nellie V., 11
San Diego, 32, 35, 39
Savings, 40
Schools, 68
Second generation, the, 68, 72
Second settlement areas, 18
Segregation, 70, 71
Self-control, 53
Siblings, 69
Sickness insurance, 50
Situation, social, 5
Skilled labor, 38
Smuggled aliens, 15
Social distance, 70
Social reorganization, 49
Social situations, 5
Social worker, 56
Spanish-Americans, 10, 11
Spanish-American Alliance, 50
Spanish immigrants, 11
Spanish-Mexicans, 11
Standards, 84
Statistics, immigration, 13-16
Status, 72
Steiner, Edward F., 55
Steiner, J. F., 23
Stereotypes, 33
Stevenson, Emma R., 93
Strike, labor, 41
Superstition, 34
Survey, industrial, 87

Taylor, Paul S., 66, 93
Teachers, 44, 68ff., 84
Teague, O. C., 50
Texas, 9
Theater, the, 60
Thomson, Charles A., 34, 67
Thrift, 47
Transient labor, 45
Tuberculosis, 33
Turnover, labor, 50
Types, Mexican, 9, 18

Union, labor, 41, 42
Unemployment, 44, 84
Unskilled labor, 12, 38, 43

Vagrancy, 55
Violence, crimes of, 54

Wages, 39
Walker, Helen W., 62, 65, 69, 98
Webb, U. S., 71
Welfare agencies, 49
Welfare, child, 68ff.
Women in industry, 43

Young, C. C., 40
Young, Pauline V., 58